Object-Oriented Systems
Analysis

YOURDON PRESS COMPUTING SERIES
Ed Yourdon, *Advisor*

Object-Oriented Systems Analysis

Modeling the World in Data

Sally Shlaer

Stephen J. Mellor

Project Technology, Inc.

YOURDON PRESS
Prentice Hall Building
Englewood Cliffs, New Jersey 07632

Library of Congress Cataloging-in-Publication Data

Shlaer, Sally.
   Object-oriented systems analysis : modeling the world in data /
Sally Shlaer, Stephen J. Mellor.
   p.   cm. — (Yourdon Press computing series)
   Bibliography: p.
   Includes index.
   ISBN 0-13-629023-X
   1. Computer software—Development.   2. System analysis.
I. Mellor, Stephen J.   II. Title.   III. Series.
QA76.76.D47S53   1988   ·
005.1—dc19

87-34049
CIP

Editorial/production supervision
  and interior design: Elaine Lynch
Cover design: Wanda Lubelska Design
Manufacturing buyer: Lorraine Fumoso

Interior line art: Todd Sallo

©1988 by Prentice-Hall, Inc.
A Division of Simon & Schuster
Englewood Cliffs, New Jersey 07632

This book can be made available to businesses
and organizations at a special discount when
ordered in large quantities.   For more information
contact:

   Prentice Hall
   Special Sales and Markets
   College Division
   Englewood Cliffs, N.J.   07632

Printed in the United States of America
10 9 8 7 6 5 4 3

ISBN 0-13-629023-X

PRENTICE-HALL INTERNATIONAL (UK) LIMITED, *London*
PRENTICE-HALL OF AUSTRALIA PTY. LIMITED, *Sydney*
PRENTICE-HALL CANADA INC., *Toronto*
PRENTICE-HALL HISPANOAMERICANA, S.A., *Mexico*
PRENTICE-HALL OF INDIA PRIVATE LIMITED, *New Delhi*
PRENTICE-HALL OF JAPAN, INC., *Tokyo*
SIMON & SCHUSTER ASIA PTE. LTD., *Singapore*
EDITORA PRENTICE-HALL DO BRASIL, LTDA., *Rio de Janeiro*

To Sarzak

In Memoriam

Contents

4 ATTRIBUTES 26

5 RELATIONSHIPS 47

6 CONSTRUCTIONS INVOLVING MANY OBJECTS 65

7 REPRESENTATION OF THE INFORMATION MODEL 76

8 TECHNIQUES 86

9 THE ROLE OF THE INFORMATION MODEL IN SYSTEM DEVELOPMENT 91

Preface

Over the past eight years, we have seen Information Modeling used in systems analysis for a large number of software development projects, including commuter train line control, election and ballot management, reagent tracking in a chemical laboratory, image management for credit card transactions, aluminum rolling mill control, electrical power monitoring and distribution, labor charge and progress tracking for a civil engineering construction project, advanced real-time graphics software, isotope separation plant control, optical disk management, and the solution of partial differential equations of mathematical physics. These projects have been presented to us under various rubrics: database modeling, expert systems, real-time process control, system software, automatic code generation, artificial intelligence, computer-integrated manufacturing, and object-oriented systems.

What do these problems have in common? Not much, other than the fact that the information models have been *moderately to spectacularly successful* in the systems analysis phase. In addition, for those projects that have now progressed well into implementation, we observe that the subsequent software development has generally been a fairly routine matter: The developers have encountered few surprises along the way.

This is, to our way of thinking, an impressive track record, both in breadth and in effect. As a result, we have come to regard information modeling as a powerful and essential skill that belongs in the tool kit of every modern software engineer.

This is easier said than accomplished. Although a tremendous amount of material has been published on semantic models, data models, and closely associated topics in the academic press, we have found few sources that comprehensively address the primary concerns of the practicing professional:

- How should one model this rule or observation?
- How can one depict a large model graphically?
- How should an information model be documented?

This book addresses these three questions. The answers have been synthe-sized from the experience of analysts in professional practice and from the profes-sional literature; in every case, they have been subjected to repeated testing and refinement in the workaday world of large, obscure, and complex systems.

In broadest terms, the three primary questions are dealt with as follows:

- The modeling rules and structures given here are based on abstraction and interpretation of the relational theory of data [Codd, 1970; Date 1977, 1986].
- The graphical Information Structure Diagram notation has its roots in the Bachman diagrams [see Martin 1977] familiar to database designers and in Entity-Relationship diagrams [Chen 1977; Tsichritzis and Lochovsky, 1982].
- The Information Model Description Documents derive from a form and or-ganization developed by John P. Lynch, whose unpublished contributions are acknowledged with the greatest pleasure.

This book evolved from a set of notes and examples on Information Modeling. Our goal then was to provide a practical, how-to view for the busy practitioner—long on examples, and light on theory. The result was a "picturebook," a childlike, Zen-like view of the technique. Feedback from a number of our colleagues in-dicated that the picturebook quality was important to its success. In this, the successor to the original picturebook, we have tried to maintain that innocent, intuitive quality.

Grateful acknowledgements are therefore due to Marianne Giovanetti, who provided the motivation for the original picturebook; to Ted Hlavac, Deborah Ohlsen, and Bill Greiman, who encouraged us to continue; and to Leon Starr for a number of original and delightful examples. Thanks also to Laurie Levin, who brought a new standard of organization and pedagogy to our material; to David Balaban, Peter Coad, Jr., Alan Hecht, Eric Vessely, Gio Wiederhold, and Ed Yourdon for numerous pertinent criticisms and suggestions; and to the staff of Prentice Hall, who supported and indulged us, despite the publication problems engendered by the picturebook format.

Special thanks go to Michael A. O'Brien, who first pointed us toward this fascinating subject matter, and who supplied the subtitle to the book. Finally, we are grateful to Project Technology, Inc. for the whole-hearted support we have received during the preparation of this work.

For training information on the method described in this book, see page 145.

Sally Shlaer
Stephen J. Mellor

Berkeley, California

Chapter 1

Why Information Modeling?

1.1 DIFFICULTIES IN SOFTWARE DEVELOPMENT

Why is it so difficult to build a large information processing system: to know exactly what we are doing as we progress through the many steps of the software development and to have at the end (on time and within budget, of course) a system that meets the user's requirements and expectations and is easy to maintain, modify, and understand?

On the basis of experience, we have identified some problems that seem to be fundamental: They arise again and again; they plague both large and small development projects. In hindsight, they can frequently be seen as major contributors to project failure. These problems are all based on information or misinformation in one way or another. How many of the following have you seen or experienced somewhere along the way?

Working Outside Your Area of Expertise. When a computer specialist gets a new client, takes a new job, or is assigned to a new project, he generally faces a new application. Frequently, the new work is entirely foreign to prior experience or formal training; instead, it involves a whole new area of expert knowledge in accounting, communications, financial reporting, processing chemicals, train control, or the like.

The problem is that suddenly there is a lot to learn, and learning about the new application takes time and effort. However, little time is typically allocated specifically for the learning, and no framework or method is laid out to assist in the learning process.

Since the programs constituting the eventual system are to be based on or compatible with expert application knowledge, we have to find a way to identify that knowledge and incorporate it into the software development process.

Multiple Vocabularies/Interdisciplinary Efforts. Large software systems generally require the integration of diverse specializations: Financial managers, auditors, engineers, operations experts, and the like must be drawn into the requirements and analysis process. In attempting to do this, one typically finds areas of partially-overlapping expert knowledge, each with separate and sometimes conflictive vocabularies. For example, a crucible to the cooling engineer is characterized in terms of heat exchange and water flow; to the vacuum system engineer, it is a vessel which must be evacuated. The same word, *crucible*, is being used for two physically distinct, though closely connected, entities. Similarly, an order in the Shipping Department is quite different from an order in Sales.

The fact that these separate vocabularies and, more significantly, their implied *separate conceptual frameworks* exist in an organization should be taken seriously: One has to assume that the subject matter is sufficiently complex that a single vocabulary could not arise through normal informal processes. As a result, real intellectual effort is required for investigating and resolving possible differences. Until this is done, any attempt at stating system requirements is bound to be troubled, since no one can be certain exactly what vocabulary has been used in the requirements statement.

Since it so frequently falls to the computer specialist to resolve these naturally-occurring conceptual discrepancies and to ferret out the assumptions behind them, a method must be provided for doing that and for verifying that it has been done correctly.

Changing Information. It is very common for the scope of a computer system—the precise functions available to an operator—to undergo change during development and even after system delivery. Similarly, it is more the rule than the exception for the set of information available to the computer to change: Process control specialists are especially familiar with the situation in which the list of sensors to be read by the computer stabilizes only after the system has been installed (if then).

This pattern of change is a reality that needs to be accommodated in our software development process.

We need to distinguish between changes that have no appreciable effect on the software development proper (in a power distribution system: whether we have seven or eight circuit breakers in a substation, for example), and those that represent major changes in function (we have now been asked to compute and optimize cost of power bought for the grid from various outside sources, for example).

Uncertainty.   When you are working outside your area of expertise, it is difficult to be sure of what you know and what you don't know. This is likely to be particularly confusing because of conflicting vocabularies, and because the normal change pattern described previously can make last month's truth into this month's falsehood. When we add these elements to our normal human propensity to get confused in the presence of a great deal of information, uncertainty abounds. These uncertainties are particularly striking in real time systems that control processes whose fundamental nature is incompletely understood—even by the experts.

It is also difficult to know what you are *expected* to know; cultural factors sometimes make it hard to expose your lack of knowledge. This can make it difficult to ask the questions that everyone has, but is afraid to ask.

What is needed is a way in which the information gathered can be exposed so that each separate "fact," contained therein, can be inspected and confirmed or refuted independently.

Faulty Expert Knowledge.   It is sometimes the case, even with systems that are already in operation, that the experts have incorrect information about how something works. In one system replacement project, we consulted with three different engineering divisions in order to determine how a particular complex of equipment worked. Three different, and fundamentally conflicting, descriptions emerged. In the end it turned out that all the experts were wrong. Each division "explained" the equipment in a way that made the aspect of the equipment for which they were responsible seem straightforward, while neglecting aspects which were the responsibility of other divisions.

What is needed is a way to capture information so that it can be checked against the reality, rather than the different, and possibly inconsistent, "user views" of reality.

Don't Know What IT Really Is.   This particularly difficult problem arises most commonly in system software development—applications such as graphics, database management software, operating systems, alarm management in real-time systems, spreadsheets, and word processing—where the problem at hand has a utility or generic nature. The intention is that the resulting software can be used for a wide variety of higher-order applications, with relatively few limitations imposed on the user.

To illustrate, consider the problem of alarm management. An "alarm" can be thought of as:

any event that generates a message that must be shown to the operator; or

the *transition of a signal* from a "normal" or "safe" state to an "abnormal" or "unsafe" state (that generates a message that must be shown to the operator); or

the fact that a signal *is in* an abnormal state.

Depending on which definition is chosen, different rules are appropriate for (1) requiring the operator to acknowledge an alarm message, (2) allowing an operator to delete the alarm message from his screen, (3) requiring the operator to take specific action in order to delete the alarm message, and (4) reprompting the operator about an alarm message that was shown to him at some time in the past. Under such circumstances, it can be difficult to formulate a satisfactory definition, since there are such a number of intertangled issues that must be resolved consistently, and *since there is no reason* a priori *to choose one definition over another.*

What we need is a method by which we can lay out candidate definitions of such conceptual entities and examine the implications of those definitions.

1.2 HOW PROJECTS GO AWRY

In our experience, failure to address the fundamental information-based problems listed above can lead to any or all of the following consequences. Fortunately, some of these consequences, or failure modes, show up relatively early in the life of a project when there is still time to take corrective action.

Floundering in Analysis.   Many systems development projects begin with an analysis phase in which a great deal of information is transmitted from the various application experts to the systems developers. However, after a time, confusion sets in due to the quantity of information the analysts must take into account and the fact that they have few tools or techniques for managing that information. A protracted period of floundering then ensues, and the schedule suffers.

Modern software engineering tools (data flow diagrams) and automated computer aids (data dictionary packages, for example) have little impact on the flounder problem, since the origin of the problem is a lack of fundamental understanding of the conceptual entities that make up the application problem. Given such understanding, the tools and aids do help; lacking it, they serve only to provide an activity in which to flounder.

Requirements Failure. It's Nobody's Job to Understand It All.   Many projects produce, as their first major deliverable, a formal statement of system requirements. The requirements document is then reviewed by a committee of experts from various departments in the organization. However, because the requirements statement contains material from so many different areas, each committee member sees himself as responsible for the quality of only a part of the specification. The responsibility for understanding the entire statement, in depth, together with all of the assumptions and conceptualizations on which it rests, is typically held by no one.

As a result, it is almost inevitable that the requirements document will later be found incomplete and/or inconsistent. It is also likely that, as these faults start to emerge, the credibility of the requirements will be so damaged that the document will come to be discounted by the system developers: The work that went into it will have been of little use.

Premature Rush to Implementation.   Because the developers' professional interests relate to computers and not to the application area *per se*, or because floundering is starting to set in, the project may terminate its efforts at understanding the application area prematurely, and move to concentrate most of its effort on design and implementation. The result can be a system that is a computer specialist's delight, employing some of the most advanced techniques of computer science, as well as the latest capabilities of the operating system, but which may be unintelligent at the application level, or lacking in needed functionality, or feature an operator interface that is poorly matched to the users' requirements.

Faults and Inconsistencies in the System.   It is traditional to assign each computer specialist the chore of producing a number of the separate programs that make up a typical system. Since the programs are not truly independent (they generally employ data to communicate information between one another), misunderstandings between the various designers about the precise meaning of a piece of data easily lead to inconsistencies and bugs in the final system.

We have had the misfortune to observe numerous projects stuck in an interminable testing and integration phase for exactly this reason. In one particular case, weeks were lost when one half of the team interpreted a *logical disk* as a single writeable surface, whereas the other half of the team thought of it as both sides of the physical disk. It is clear that in a large programming team it will be difficult to find and resolve all problems of this sort.

Similarly, in real-time control systems, if the computer specialists do not have an accurate picture of how a complex of equipment operates, the programs that interact with that equipment are bound to produce unexpected events in the plant being controlled.

Unintelligent System.   Consider a system which monitors and controls an electric power distribution network. An unintelligent system would know only about the existence and the sensed states of each circuit breaker, and it would be able to show to an operator whether each circuit breaker is open or closed. In this system, it would be up to the operator to figure out what this all means in terms of where power is being supplied in the network. Contrast this to a system that is also aware of the cables. If the system knows which circuit breaker is used to transfer power between which cables—the connectivity of the network—it can then tell whether or not any particular cable is hot and predict the likely consequences of opening or closing a particular circuit breaker. Note that the cables are not controllable (and may not be equipped with voltage sensors). It is only the fact that the system is aware of their existence and their relationship to the circuit breakers that makes the second system more intelligent.

Clearly, for any given set of sensors, the more application knowledge that can be built into the system, the more intelligent the system will be. It can provide more information upon which operators can base decisions and it can do more work without the guidance of the operator (if a breaker fails to open, the system can trace through the network and open an electrically-adjacent breaker, for example).

The extent to which the system exploits the information available through the sensors, taking on the character of an "expert system," is often limited by the application knowledge that the computer specialists are able to obtain and assimilate.

Similar situations also occur in commercial systems. Consider a brokerage house that fails to distinguish between the notion of a customer and of an account. Although many customers may have only a single account, some may have several: for example, an IRA account and an ordinary account. Any information that needs to be distributed to customers (advertising a new service, for example) will be distributed several times to each customer with more than one account. In a company with a large customer base, the unnecessary costs incurred can be considerable.

1.3 INFORMATION MODELING AS AN ANSWER

In our experience, information modeling provides a powerful and specific cure for the project failure modes just described. It works because it meets the requirements of Section 1.1, and it does so in a simple and effective way. But what is an Information Model exactly?

Physically, an **Information Model** consists of an organization and a graphical notation suitable for describing and defining the vocabulary and conceptualization of a problem domain.The primary exposition of the Information Model is in highly structured text; This is where the semantics of the problem domain are stated. The graphical notation is used to provide an integrated overview of the whole.

The model focuses on the real world under study; identifies, classifies and abstracts what is in the problem; and organizes the information into a formal structure. Similar "things," or instances, in the problem are identified and abstracted as *objects*; characteristics of these instances are abstracted as *attributes*; and reliable associations between the instances are abstracted as *relationships*. The abstraction process requires that each instance be subject to and conform to the well-defined and explicitly stated rules or policy of the problem domain.

Moving up a level, we can say that an information model is a *thinking tool* used to aid in the formalization of knowledge. It helps us work out how we want to think about a problem: the terms we need to define, the assumptions we make in selecting those terms, and the consistency of our definitions and assumptions.

1.4 WHEN TO USE INFORMATION MODELING IN THE SOFTWARE DEVELOPMENT PROCESS

In our experience, it is advantageous to initiate the software development project with the construction of an Information Model of the application problem. Following this, other analysis steps (data flow diagrams, state transition diagrams, formal requirements work, and the like) can be applied when appropriate to the problem.

Separating the construction of the model from other tasks in the software development makes explicit the work of acquiring the expert application knowledge and bringing it into the software development; as such, this work can receive the serious attention it requires for success.

In the lead-off position in the application analysis phase, the model provides a place to hang the large volume of information which would previously have inundated the analyst. In addition, the formal and systematic nature of the model acts to expose inconsistencies and gaps, thereby guiding the inquiry.

Once a draft model has been produced, it can be reviewed by the various applications experts so that the accuracy of the information, as received by the software development staff, can be confirmed. At this stage, it is common to find that a large number of miscommunications have occurred; these can be weeded out quickly before they become established in the project's store of common mis-knowledge.

The information model then proceeds through any necessary revisions, each time serving to record the information that is known and, at the same time, serving as an instrument of communication among all the disciplines that are involved in the work. This has been found to be extremely effective in detecting and resolving the discrepancies between the various divergent views originally presented to the software developers.

At this point, the software developers have a clear understanding of the problem under analysis, and further steps in the development life cycle can be made from a firm basis. These steps are described in Chapter 9.

1.5 PREVIEW

The remainder of this book is concerned with learning how to build an information model. We begin in Chapter 2 with a intuitive "right-brain oriented" presentation of the basic concepts, cast primarily in pictures. This is followed in Chapters 3 through 6 by a complete, example-based presentation of the modeling language and formalism. Chapter 7 deals with documentation issues, and provides a summary of the graphic notation developed earlier. Suggestions and techniques for obtaining the raw knowledge to be formalized appear in Chapter 8, while Chapter 9 discusses how information modeling fits into the larger picture of software development. Finally, the appendices contain two examples of fully-developed information models.

Chapter 2

Basic Ideas

The world is full of **things**.

We abstract like things and call the abstractions **objects**.

In forming such abstractions, we choose to ignore most of the things in the world. The remaining things are grouped according to concepts and perceptions we hold about what it means to be "like."

Our ideas of what constitute appropriate criteria for establishing likenesses depend on the purposes we have in mind.

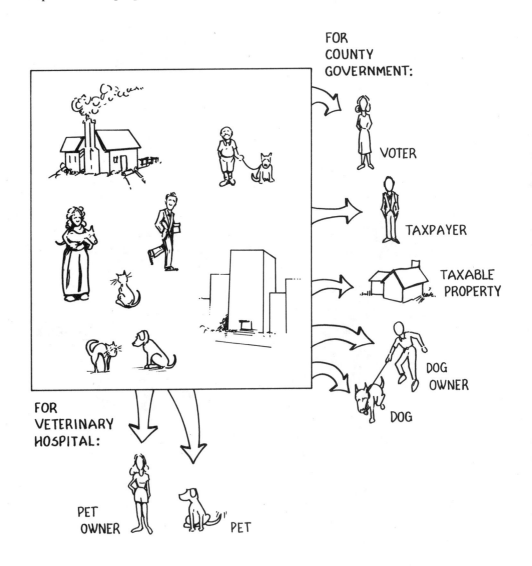

We can represent an abstract object by an empty **table**.

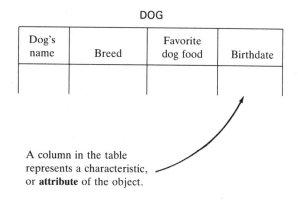

DOG

Dog's name	Breed	Favorite dog food	Birthdate

A column in the table
represents a characteristic,
or **attribute** of the object.

The table can be filled in to represent the real-world things from which the object
was abstracted.

DOG

Dog's name	Breed	Favorite dog food	Birthdate
Boris	St.Bernard	Canned	Jan 81
Fifi	Poodle	Dry	May 77
Rover	Mix	Chicken	July 83

We represent a particular
instance of the object
—a single real world thing—
by a row in the table.

We choose attributes which support the ideas of likeness we had in mind when we abstracted the object.

For the county government offices:

LICENSED DOG

Licence number	Dog name	Breed	Sex	Owner name	License date

DOG OWNER

Owner name	Address

TAXABLE PROPERTY

Property number	Assessed value	Taxes paid until

PROPERTY OWNER

Owner name	Address

For the veterinary hospital:

PET

Pet name	Species	Breed	Sex	Date of Birth	Weight

PET OWNER

Owner name	Address	Account balance

There are **relationships** between objects,

which show up as attributes.

LICENSED DOG

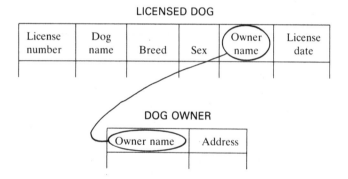

The name of this relationship is "OWNS," as in

Dog Owner OWNS Dogs.

The idea of an **Information Model** is to describe the

- objects
- attributes of those objects
- relationships between objects

which are interesting for the problem at hand. Chapters 3 through 6 tell how to do this in a precise and consistent manner.

Chapter 3

Objects

3.1 DEFINITION OF OBJECT

Definition: An *object* is an abstraction of a set of real-world things such that:

- all of the real-world things in the set—the instances—have the same characteristics
- all instances are subject to and conform to the same rules

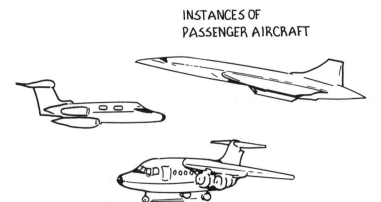

INSTANCES OF
PASSENGER AIRCRAFT

PASSENGER
AIRCRAFT
(OBJECT)

CHARACTERISTICS OF
PASSENGER AIRCRAFT

- manufacturer
- type
- serial number
- passenger
  capacity

What does this definition imply?

. . . all have the same characteristics: If you make a table representation of an object and you enter the instances from which you abstracted the object into the table. . . .

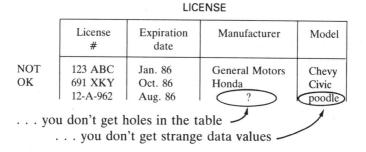

LICENSE

	License #	Expiration date	Manufacturer	Model
NOT OK	123 ABC	Jan. 86	General Motors	Chevy
	691 XKY	Oct. 86	Honda	Civic
	12-A-962	Aug. 86	?	poodle

. . . you don't get holes in the table

. . . you don't get strange data values

. . . all follow the same rules: We want to be able to define simple operations on the data that are easy to understand and easy to get right. Let's say we want to define an operation that makes a re-registration packet. Using the License object above, we would need to:

(a) Find all instances which have "expiration date" 2 months from the current date

(b) For each row, if manufacturer = "null," then print a dog license re-registration packet with a blank rabies vaccination certification, otherwise print a vehicle re-registration packet.

What we're trying to avoid is the branching logic inherent in (b). This simple example gives only a hint of the additional complexity which develops when two different kinds of "things" are put into the same table. The point is, there is one set of rules (law, policy, etc.) that applies to dogs and a different set of rules that applies to cars. Every operation must account for this by asking "which kind of thing is this?" Further, if one were later to add fishing licenses to the same table, *all* the existing operations would become invalid and would have to be redefined.

3.2 IDENTIFYING OBJECTS

Identifying objects is pretty easy to do. Start out by focussing on the problem at hand and ask yourself, "What are the *things* in this problem?" Most of the things are likely to fall into the following five categories.

1. Tangible things
2. Roles

3. Incidents
4. Interactions
5. Specifications

Note that these categories aren't offered as a classification system for objects but as a set of "starter ideas" for finding objects in a new problem.

3.2.1 Tangible Things

These are the easiest objects to find. Given the appropriate problem, how could you miss an object such as:

airplane   circuit breaker
pipe support   magnet
nuclear reactor   power supply
racehorse   vehicle
national landmark   book

NUCLEAR POWER PLANT

CHEMICAL VESSEL

TRAIN

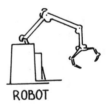

ROBOT

3.2.2 Roles Played by Persons or Organizations

This category is best described by examples:

doctor   owner
patient   tenant
broker   account holder
client   department
employee   taxpayer
supervisor   trustee

Frequently, if you have one role object, you will have others also. This comes about when role objects are being used to distinguish between different roles played by the same or different people (obviously enough); hence, one would expect to find Doctor, Nurse, Patient, and similar objects in a model describing the operation of a hospital. This set of objects would allow for the case of a nurse who is currently a patient in the hospital.

3.2.3 Incidents

Incident objects are used to represent an occurrence or event: something which happens at a specific time. Some reasonable incident objects are:

    flight
    accident
    performance (of a play, etc.)
    event (in a nuclear physics experiment)
    system crash
    service call (appliance repair)

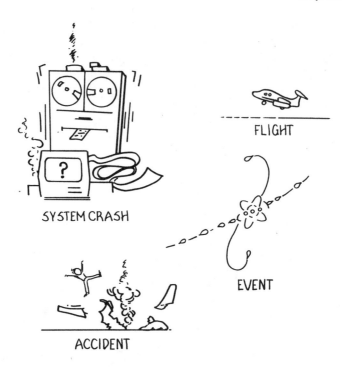

SYSTEM CRASH

FLIGHT

EVENT

ACCIDENT

3.2.4 Interactions

Interaction objects generally have a "transaction" or "contract" quality, and relate to two or more other objects in the model.   Examples are:

> purchase (related to buyer, seller, and thing purchased)
> marriage (related to man and woman)

Interaction objects may also come up when modeling geometrical or topological systems: an electrical network, the piping in a refinery, or the trackwork of a railroad.

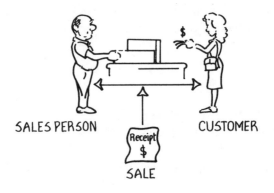

SALES PERSON

CUSTOMER

SALE

3.2.5 Specifications

Specification objects frequently show up in inventory or manufacturing applications. They have the quality of a standard or a definition. For example:

REFRIGERATOR MODEL

The specification:
What it means to be a
Model 172

Model #	Cubic feet	Power rating	. . .
169A	10		
172	12		

It is generally true that when you have a specification object, you will also have another object that represents instances of things that meet the specifications.

REFRIGERATOR

Tangible things that meet
the specification

Serial #	Model #	Present location
123961	169A	shipping department
123962	169A	quality control
161962	172	Joe's Appliance Store
161921	172	shipping department

The "instances object" need not represent something tangible: For example, we could have Policy Types (the specification object) and Insurance Policies (the instances).

3.3 OBJECT DESCRIPTIONS

An *object description* is a short, informative statement which allows one to tell, with certainty, whether or not a particular real world thing is an instance of the object as conceptualized in the information model.

An object description must be provided for each object in the model. Here are some pointers which we have found helpful in producing good object descriptions. The pointers are illustrated, for the most part, by extracts from an object description for the Passenger Aircraft object.

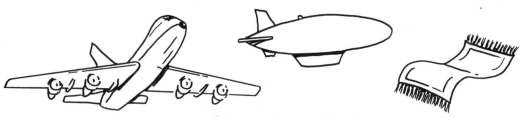

Instances of Passenger Aircraft

Object Description Guidelines

Basis of Abstraction: Inclusion Criteria.   Describe the class of real-world things abstracted by the object, emphasizing the ways in which instances of the object are alike (that is, inclusion criteria).

> *Object:*   Passenger Aircraft
>
> *Description:* A Passenger Aircraft is an aircraft which has been fitted with seats and other equipment suitable for supporting safe and comfortable travel by paying passengers.

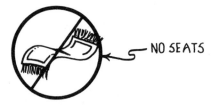

Basis of Abstraction: Exclusion Criteria.   Establish exclusion criteria if there are instances that are *not* being abstracted into this object.

> A certain quality of finish and decor is required of passenger aircraft used by this airline.   As a result, planes fitted out in a utilitarian style (such as small freighters used to transport parts from one maintenance center to another) are not considered to be passenger aircraft, even though they are equipped with seats.

Context of Object.   Explain how the object relates to other objects in the model.

> At least one Passenger Aircraft is assigned to each Scheduled Flight.

This guideline is especially important when the meaning of the object requires the presence of another object.

> A Supervisor is responsible for assigning and evaluating the work of the Employees under his supervision.
> A Supervisor must have at least one Employee working for him.

Background Information.   Sometimes a certain amount of background information enhances the object description.

> Generally, only one passenger aircraft is assigned to a scheduled flight.
> If, however, unusual events (strikes at competing airlines, heavy snow-

fall, and the like) have caused a large number of customers to be stranded at a particular airport, a second passenger aircraft may be assigned.

World Statements vs. Model Statements.   In writing an object description, one needs to make statements about the reality being formalized in the model as well as statements about the model constructs themselves.   To allow the reader to distinguish between these two classes of statements, we have found it helpful to establish a typographical convention: Use an initial capital letter for all words of an object name, lower case when referring to instances in the real world.

Technical Writing Standards.   Finally, standard technical writing practices apply to object descriptions: An object description should be written in short declarative sentences using the present tense.   Avoid vague or ambiguous terms.

There are a number of further examples of object descriptions contained in the appendices.   Those that we judge most successful preserve the theme of the information as a reflection and abstraction of reality.

It is a good idea to start drafting object descriptions early in the modeling process: This will frequently tell you if you are getting off the track.

3.4 NAMING OBJECTS

A good choice of names for the objects will contribute significantly to the readability and understandability of the information model.   Strive for names which are clear, direct, and honest.   This is not always easy.

In general, we prefer to name an object in the model with the common name used for instances of the object in the real world.   Unfortunately, this often turns out to be difficult.   Unless the organization involved has been through a terminology formalization process in the recent past, one is likely to find:

- a single common name being used to refer to two or more different things
- two or more common names being used to refer to the same thing
- a number of circumstances in which it appears that both things are going on simultaneously.

Although this can be very confusing for the poor analysts (namely, us), it leads to less confusion in the organization than one might expect.   This is because:

- Most terminology references take place in ordinary conversation, which supplies context for each such reference.
- Many terminology references are exchanged between application experts—people who have large amounts of special knowledge in and context for the subject at hand.

• Human beings are extremely adept in using context information for establishing meaning.

However, when it becomes necessary to transfer the special application knowledge to experts in a different area (to computer specialists, for example) imprecise context-dependent terminology begins to cause problems.

The information model can be dramatically helpful in exposing and resolving these problems. For this reason, it is useful to regard it as a dictionary in which each name has only one meaning.

Against this background, we offer the following suggestions in naming objects.

Common Names Preferred. Use common names where these are, or can be made, well-defined.

> OK: Signaling Unit
> Better: Traffic Light
>
> OK: Part Transporter
> Better: Conveyor Belt

Strong Names. Use strong, everyday words with extended meanings in preference to vague, unnecessarily technical, or esoteric terms.

Object Description: A room, closet, or defined warehouse area used to store . . .

> Not too good: Storage Environment
> Better: Room

Object Description: A cupboard, refrigerator, set of open shelves, or freezer used to store . . .

> Not too good: Storage Location
> Better: Cabinet

Same Dimension Names. Use names that contrast in the same dimension.

> Not good: High Voltage Power Supply
>   Continuous Power Supply
>
> Better: Pulsed Power Supply
>   Continuous Power Supply

Precise Names. Append adjectives to common short names to make the short names more precise.

Object Description: A room, closet, or defined warehouse area where inventory items are stored.

Basic name: Room

Precise name: Storeroom

Names Based on Essential Nature.   Use made-up names, even if they are lengthy, if they get at the essential character of the object better than more customary, but less precise terms.

Object Description: A piece of territory, not necessarily contiguous, which is defined by the intersection of all election districts. As a consequence of the mechanism by which a territory is defined, all voters residing in the territory receive identical ballots for any particular election.

Common name: Precinct (or Precinct-Split)

Better: Smallest Territorial Unit

Content-Based Names.   Name the object by its information content, not by the form commonly used to carry information.

Object Description: A person legally entitled to operate a motor vehicle.

Bad: Driver's License

Good: Licensed Driver

(If it really were a Driver's License, the description would read "a little piece of paper, about 2.25 by 3.25 inches, bearing an identifying number...")

Avoid Abused Words.   And finally, avoid "abused words" in naming your objects—words that have many meanings or great context dependence. Exactly what constitutes an abused word depends a great deal on the audience for your information model, but the following are classic examples:

account	operation
order	schedule
task	part
form	assembly

3.5 TESTING OBJECTS

When you first start identifying objects in a new problem area, you are likely to pick up a few things that appear to be objects when, in fact, they are not. Here are some tests which will help you reject these false objects. Note that some of the tests are based on the object descriptions.

3.5.1 Uniformity Test

This test is based on the definition of an object. Think of the instances—the things you would write in rows in a table representing this object. *Each instance must have the same set of characteristics and be subject to the same rules.* (Interpret "rules" liberally: laws, organizational policies, laws of physics, custom, and so forth.)

This test rejects a License object representing vehicle licenses, dog licenses, and fishing licenses.

3.5.2 More-Than-a-Name Test

Every object has attributes. If a putative object cannot be described by attributes—it has no characteristics other than its name—it is probably an attribute of something else (and not an object at all).

> Not OK: social security number
> (attribute of person)
>
> Not OK: address
>
> OK: Person
>
> OK: Social Security Account

3.5.3 The OR Test

If the inclusion criteria stated in the object description use the word "or" in a significant way, you probably don't have an object, but a bunch of conglomerated ideas instead.

> Not OK: The drawing object represents an engineering drawing under formal revision control or the pictures my little girl made in kindergarten.
>
> OK: The drawing object represents an engineering drawing or sketch under formal revision control.

The cure requires one to separate, as separate objects, the classes of things which have gotten mixed together.

3.5.4 More-Than-a-List Test

If the inclusion criteria stated in the object description amount only to a list of all the specific instances, you probably don't really have an object.

Not OK: A Decadent Food is a croissant, a cappuccino, a chocolate pie, a vanilla eclair, or an ice cream cone.

OK: A Decadent Food is an addictive food which has a severely unhealthy effect. Every decadent food has an ecstasy rating and a death index.

A failure of this test generally indicates that there is insufficient basis for abstraction of the object from its instances.

Chapter 4

Attributes

4.1 DEFINITION OF ATTRIBUTE

Definition: An *attribute* is the abstraction of a *single* characteristic possessed by all the entities that were, themselves, abstracted as an object.

The goal is to obtain a set of attributes that are

- complete—they capture all information pertinent to the object being defined;
- fully factored—each attribute captures a separate aspect of the object abstraction; and
- mutually independent—the attributes take on their values independently of one another.

Example: Suppose we are trying to characterize the customers of a company supplying a supported software package. This characterization will form the foundation of a database to be used by various departments in the company which must supply services to the customers.

The company policy has been expressed as:

There are four types of customers. A *regular* customer is entitled to run the software, receives new revisions as they are released, is allowed to call on the Technical Support

Department for help with bugs or operating problems, and receives the monthly newsletter. A *provisional* customer receives the same services as a regular customer, but doesn't get revisions. A *non-profit* customer is entitled to run only a single specified version of the software (the one shipped to him at the time he became a customer), but receives no other services. A *special* customer gets the newsletter and nothing more.

A database is to be constructed to capture the information required for supporting the services described above, including the customer's name, his address, and the version number of the software he is running. As a prelude to designing the database, determine the information structure intrinsic to this problem.

A poor solution: This solution is based on a Customer object:

Customer Name	Address	Customer Type	Version

where the legal values of Customer Type are "regular," "provisional," "non-profit," and "special."

This is considered a poor solution because the attributes Customer Type and Version are not mutually independent: If Customer Type is "special," we know that the value for the Version attribute must be "none."

Another, separate flaw is that the information about whether or not to send revisions and newsletters is combined in the same attribute, so the attributes are not fully factored.

A better solution: In this solution, the Customer object is defined as follows:

Customer Name	Address	Newsletter Service?	Send Revision?	Phone Service?	Version Running?

where we allow the Version Running attribute to take on the value "none," in addition to all the legal version numbers.

By drafting the code required to do a small support task—printing the labels for mailing the revision media, for example—you can see how much simpler the code will be if the database is structured according to our "better solution." This is not a coincidence. Basically, the rules that capture a single aspect of the object in a single attribute translate, in the code, to the checking of a single attribute for a single data value (a "yes" value for Send Revision, in this case).

4.2 NOTATION

There are a number of different notations available for showing an object together with its attributes.

First an empty table:

CUSTOMER					
Customer Name	Address	Newsletter Service?	Send Revisions?	Phone Service?	Version Running

An equivalent graphical form is:

CUSTOMER

. Customer name
. Address
. Newsletter service
. Send revisions
. Phone service
. Version running

An equivalent textual form:

Customer (Customer Name, Address, Newsletter Service, Send Revisions, Phone Service, Version Running)

An expansive graphical form that you may encounter in the literature looks like this:

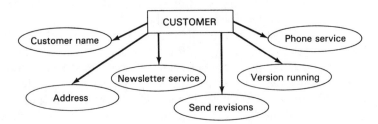

All of the above forms show an object together with all its attributes. If you want to talk about a single attribute, a good form to use is <object>.<attribute>, as in:

Customer.Address,
Customer.Version Running,

and the like.

4.3 FINDING AND CLASSIFYING ATTRIBUTES

Attributes can be identified by referring to:

- the real-world instances that were abstracted to become the object: What kinds of characteristics do *all* the instances possess?
- the object description: What information would I need to know about a real-world entity to tell if it is an instance of this object?

The attributes that you identify will fall into three categories, depending on the kind of information that each captures. The attribute categories are

Descriptive attributes: intrinsic characteristics of the object
Naming attributes: arbitrary names and labels
Referential attributes: facts which tie an instance of one object to an instance of another object

4.3.1 Descriptive Attributes

Descriptive attributes provide facts intrinsic to each instance of an object.

AIRCRAFT

- aircraft ID #
- altitude
- longitude
- latitude
- pilot license # (R)
- airplane name

The *altitude* of airplane N3172A is 10,000 feet.
The *latitude* of airplane N3172A is 25.23 degrees.
The *longitude* of airplane N3172A is 30.44 degrees.

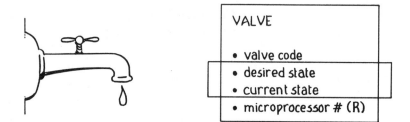

VALVE

- valve code
- desired state
- current state
- microprocessor # (R)

The *desired state* of valve 47B is CLOSED.
The *current state* of valve 47B is OPEN.

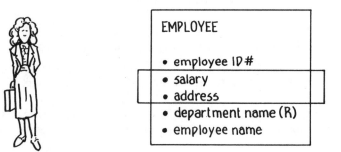

EMPLOYEE

- employee ID #
- salary
- address
- department name (R)
- employee name

The *salary* of employee 3126 is $2,000 per month.
The *address* of employee 3126 is 125 Cragmont, Berkeley, CA.

4.3.2 Naming Attributes

Naming attributes provide facts about the arbitrary labels and names carried by each instance of an object. In each of the following examples, note that you can change the names or labels of each instance of the object without changing anything else: That is, I can re-number an airplane, but it is still the same airplane.

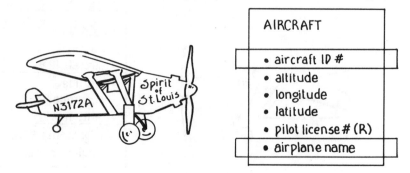

AIRCRAFT

- aircraft ID #
- altitude
- longitude
- latitude
- pilot license # (R)
- airplane name

The aircraft whose *aircraft ID* is N3172A, and whose *airplane name* is The Spirit of St. Louis.

VALVE

- valve code
- desired state
- current state
- microprocessor # (R)

The valve whose *valve code* is 47B.

EMPLOYEE

- employee ID #
- salary
- address
- department name (R)
- employee name

Mary Jones
3126

The employee whose *employee ID#* is 3126. Her *employee name* is Mary Jones.

4.3.3 Referential Attributes

Referential attributes capture the facts which tie an instance of one object to an instance of another object.

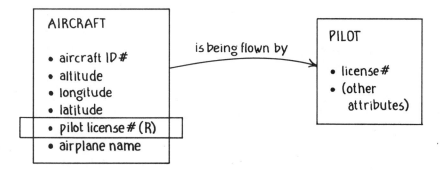

AIRCRAFT

- aircraft ID #
- altitude
- longitude
- latitude
- pilot license # (R)
- airplane name

is being flown by

PILOT

- license #
- (other attributes)

The airplane N3172A is being flown by the pilot whose license number is U77-34.

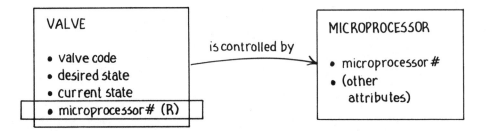

The valve 47B is controlled by microprocessor 11.

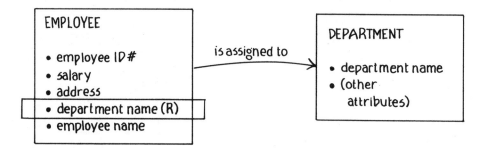

The employee 3126 is assigned to the Quality Assurance Department.

4.4 IDENTIFIERS

Definition: A set of one or more attributes which uniquely distinguishes each instance of an object is an *identifier* for that object.

An identifier is sometimes called a "candidate key."

To make a graphical rendition of your model more understandable, we suggest marking the attributes comprising an identifier with an asterisk, as has been done in the illustrations to follow.

Each employee is assigned a separate employee ID#. Employee.Employee ID# IS an identifier for the Employee object.

Employee.Employee Name is NOT an identifier (since two employees can certainly have the same name).

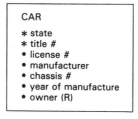

AIRCRAFT

* * aircraft ID#
* • altitude
* • longitude
* • latitude
* • pilot license # (R)
* • airplane name

Each aircraft is assigned a unique ID number by a central agency. Aircraft.Aircraft ID is therefore an identifier for the Aircraft object.

Aircraft.Airplane Name is NOT an identifier, since two people can choose to name their planes the same thing.

An identifier may consist of multiple attributes.

CAR

* * state
* * title #
* • license #
* • manufacturer
* • chassis #
* • year of manufacture
* • owner (R)

An object may have several identifiers (each of which consists of one or more attributes).

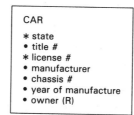

CAR

* * state
* * title #
* • license #
* • manufacturer
* • chassis #
* • year of manufacture
* • owner (R)

CAR

* * state
* • title #
* * license #
* • manufacturer
* • chassis #
* • year of manufacture
* • owner (R)

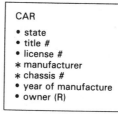

CAR

* • state
* • title #
* • license #
* * manufacturer
* * chassis #
* • year of manufacture
* • owner (R)

In this case, one must select a favorite identifier to be denoted by asterisks on the graphical model. When using the textual form, you can underline the preferred identifier:

Car (State, Title Number, License Number, <u>Manufacturer, Chassis Number,</u>
      Year of Manufacture, Owner)

Every object must have at least one identifier. We note the identifiers of an object with the object description:

```
Object:  CAR
CAR (state, license number, title number,
       manufacturer, chassis number, model, year)


Identifiers:  state + title
              state + license number
              manufacturer + chassis number


Description: _____
_____
_____
_____
_____
```

All three kinds of attributes can be used to compose an identifier.

```
Object:  AIRPORT
AIRPORT (airport code, latitude, longitude, city)


Identifiers:  airport code  ◄──────────────── naming
              latitude + longitude                attribute
                                              ── descriptive
Description: _____     attribute
_____
_____
```

```
┌─────────────────────────────────────────────┐
│                                               │
│  Object: ROBOT                                │
│  ROBOT (manufacturer, serial number, model,   │
│           date last inspected)                │
│                                               │
│                                               │
│  Identifiers: manufacturer + serial number ◄──────── naming
│                                       ╲                  attribute
│                                        ╲─────────────── referential
│  Description: _____              attribute
│  _____      │
│  _____      │
│  _____      │
│                                               │
 ╲╱──╲────╱──╲───╱─╲──╱─╲──╱──╲──╱──╲
```

Note that the idea of a naming attribute is different from that of an identifier (although naming attributes are frequently used in identifiers).

4.5 ATTRIBUTE DESCRIPTIONS

An *attribute description* is a short, informative description that tells how the formal attribute reflects the real-world characteristic of interest. Such an attribute description is required for every attribute in the information model. Some suggestions for preparing the attribute descriptions are given below together with a few examples.

4.5.1 Describing the Descriptive Attributes

The attribute description for a descriptive attribute states what real-world characteristic, possessed by all instances of the object, is being captured in the model by this attribute.

┌───┐
│   │
│   *Attribute:* Driver.Address   │
│   │
│   *Description:* This address is the address at which the driver receives mail. │
│   It can be a legal or common-use street address recognized by the U.S. │
│   Post Office, or a post office box.   │
│   │
└───┘

Attribute: Magnet.Desired Current

Description: This attribute reflects the setting desired for the magnet current.

Attribute: Radiation Worker.Dose to Date

Description: The radiation dose received by each worker is monitored by film badges, personal dosimeters, and similar devices. The dose received is recorded and accumulated during the year. This data is used to control work assigments so that workers do not receive more than the dosage allowed per year.

4.5.2 Describing Naming Attributes

The attribute description for a naming attribute should specify the form of the name (if relevant); the organization that assigns, registers, or controls the names (if relevant); and the extent to which the attribute can be used as a part of an identifier.

Attribute: Magnet.Name

Description: Magnet names are assigned by the beamline designers. The names begin with a B (for bending magnets) or F (for focussing magnets). A numeric "magnet number" of two or three digits follows the initial letter.

Note that there is no firm convention for handling leading zeros: B6 and B06 can denote the same magnet, depending on which drawing or document is consulted. For the purpose of formalizing this attribute, leading zeros will be suppressed.

Magnet.Name does not identify a magnet uniquely: There are magnets denoted F12 on both the North line (drawing EM-124396-B) and on the West dog-leg (EM-C-69125). There could be other duplications; an exhaustive check has not been made.

Sometimes it is necessary to invent a naming attribute to ensure that an object has an identifier.   If so, the fact should be noted in the attribute description.

Attribute: Sump Pump.ID

Description: This attribute has been constructed for this model to provide an identifier for the Sump Pump object.   Sump Pump IDs are of the form SP <digit><digit>.

4.5.3 Describing Referential Attributes

The attribute description for a referential attribute states the relationship being captured in the model by the referential attribute.   Assignment of referential attributes to objects is discussed in more detail in Chapter 5.

Attribute: Magnet.Power Supply

Description: This attribute captures the name of the power supply which powers the magnet.

This attribute formalizes the relationship Magnet IS POWERED BY Power Supply.

4.6 DOMAINS

Definition: The set of values an attribute can take on constitutes its *domain*.

Attribute	Domain
Power Supply.Polarity	positive, negative
Car Owner.Address	any street address recognized by the Post Office
Dog.Breed	poodle, afghan, mixed breed, . . .
Cryochamber.Temperature	0-500 Kelvin

A definition of the domain must be provided for each attribute. You can define the domain in several ways, depending on the category of the attribute.

4.6.1 Domains of Descriptive Attributes

Specify the domain of a descriptive attribute in one of the following ways:

Enumeration. Give an explicit list of all the possibilities.

> *Attribute:*
>   Power Supply.Interlock
>
> *Description:* ～～～～～～
>
> *Domain:* [ok | tripped]

Citation. A document which acts as the official source of the possibilities may be cited.

> *Attribute:*
>   Employee.Job Class
>
> *Description:* ～～～～～～
>
> *Domain:* See Corporate Supervisors' Manual, Part 7, for current list of job classes.

Acceptance Rule. State a rule for determinining if a value asserted should be accepted as a legal value of the attribute.

> *Attribute:*
>   Dog.Breed
>
> *Description:* ～～～～～～
>
> *Domain:* Any breed name stated by the dog owner

Range. State the units, and the aceptable range of values for the attribute.

> *Attribute:*
>   Magnet.Desired Current
>
> *Description:* ～～～～～
>
> *Domain:* 0 - 300 amps.

4.6.2 Domains for Naming Attributes

The domain for a naming attribute can be specified

as **"See Above"**. This form is used
when the attribute description essen-
tially defines the legal values.

```
Attribute:
    Magnet.Name

Description: ~~~~~~~~~

Domain: See above.
```

by **Enumeration**.

```
Attribute:
    Air Terminal.Name

Description: ~~~~~~~~~

Domain: North, East, Freight
```

by **Citation of** official source documents.

```
Attribute:
    Circuit Breaker.ID

Description: ~~~~~~~~~

Domain: See substation construc-
tion drawings
```

4.6.3 Domains for Referential Attributes

The domain of a referential attribute is necessarily the same as the domain of (a
part of) an identifier of another object in the model. Hence, the domain is always
specified by referring to another domain. This will be presented in greater detail
in Chapter 5.

"Same As"

```
Attribute:
    Magnet.Power Supply

Description: ~~~~~~~~~

Domain: Same as Power Sup-
ply.ID
```

4.6.4 Further Points on Domain Definition

Are Null Values of an Attribute OK?   Yes, if what is being indicated by the null value is "we don't know yet" (temporarily missing data) or "none".   If this is your intention, though, it might be better to define the domain to *include* values "unknown" and "none".

If, however, the null value is trying to indicate "not applicable", it is not legal, but is symptomatic of a deeper problem.   Chances are that you really have two objects which are not yet being distinguished: For example, a Person object with an attribute Number of Pregnancies.

Contrast this with a Car object which has as an attribute the type of air conditioner installed in it.   If a particular car has no air conditioner, the value of the attribute could be defined to be Null (meaning None).   Note that this is different from the first example because the car *could* have an air conditioner installed; it just happens that this particular car does not.

Syntax vs. Semantics.   Define domains in terms of the meaning of the data (the semantics), not the form (syntax) of the data.

> Not OK: Floating point number
> OK: 0–300 amps
>
> Not OK: 1–50 alphanumeric characters
> OK: client name .

4.7 FORMALIZING THE CONCEPT OF TABLE

There are a number of definitions and rules—the so-called normalization rules— which are used to define the relational model of data.   These rules can be viewed from two perspectives.   The first focusses on the form of data in databases: From this perspective, the rules tell how to set up tables so that there is little redundancy in the data—that is, the amount of data required to store a certain information content is minimized.

The second perspective (the one most natural to us) looks at the normalization rules as statements about the repertoire of forms that we use in our model (the fact that we are using tables, for example), and the meaning we imply whenever we use a form in a particular manner.   What are we really saying when we assign an attribute to an object?

This section discusses the rules in which the relational model is usually presented.   More extensive discussions can be found in the database texts by Date and Ullman.   (See Appendix C).

4.7.1 Regular Tables

First Rule: One instance of an object has exactly one value for each attribute. (There is one and only one data element at each row-column intersection.)

This rule forbids the "repeating group" construct found in some databases.

	NOT OK	Smith	Rover	100 Canine Court
			RinTinTin	
			Sarzak	
		Jones	Lassie	6 Dogwood Lane

This rule forbids true holes in the table.

	Owner	Model	Manufacturer	License #
NOT OK	Brown	Sedan	Ford	16923A
	Green	Van	Chevrolet	23004C
	Jones	Collie		29-A-101

The First Rule is really a definition of "table" or, in the terminology of the relational model, *relation* (not to be confused with "relationship," which is a separate concept). It provides for a table with the properties we want:

- Each instance of an object occupies exactly one row.
- The instances you record in a table are so uniform that you don't get holes.

4.7.2 Atomic Attributes

Second Rule: Attributes must contain no internal structure.

This is another expression of the requirement for fully-factored attributes. The rule forbids such tables as:

Not OK:

Name	Sex/breed
Lassie	F-Collie
Laddie	M-Collie
Fifi	F-Poodle

OK:

Name	Sex	Breed
Lassie	F	Collie
Laddie	M	Collie
Fifi	F	Poodle

DATA
  BASE
    WIZARD

If your model conforms to both the First and Second Rules, you can say that the model is in First Normal Form.

4.7.3 Coping with Non-Atomic Attributes

The Second Rule points to a common problem area: names of equipment and certain kinds of "created entities."

Example:

A Problem Report Numbering Scheme. This scheme is used to help a utility company keep track of currently unresolved equipment and procedural problems arising in power plants.

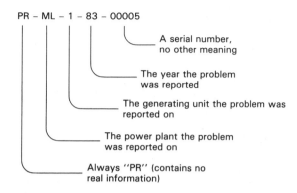

The hyphens in the name have no meaning. They are used to make the problem numbers more readable.

Assume that a formal problem reporting procedure has been in place for several years. This procedure has used non-automated methods for keeping track of the problems and their status. Now we want to build a database to make the situation more managable.

The Problem Reporting staff is expecting a database that looks something like:

Problem Number	Description	Department Responsible For Fixing	Date Fixed

plus a set of reports which sort or select on year, power plant, unit, and so forth. The information required to produce the reports is buried inside the problem number.

A better reflection of the *concept* of Reported Problem is this:

REPORTED PROBLEM

Power Plant	Unit	Year Reported	Serial Number	Description	Department Responsible For Fixing

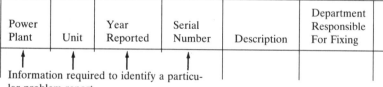

Information required to identify a particular problem report

This formulation allows you to construct the Problem Number from the information on which it is based, according to the rules given earlier for assigning problem numbers. The required reports will be easy to produce, since the information on which they are based is already broken out by the table structure itself.

A potential difficulty emerges when you learn that the rules for assigning the Problem Numbers may not have been uniformly observed. Perhaps a Unit number of zero is sometimes used to indicate that all units at the power plant are involved, or a suffix is added to the Year Reported field to indicate the severity of the problem. Bearing in mind that we have several file drawers of accumulated Problem Report

Forms, it may be difficult to determine exactly what conventions were observed at various times in the past. In such a case, we would prefer a model like this . . .

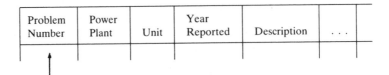

in which the Problem Number is treated as an arbitrary (structureless) name. While this will cause considerable redundancy in the database, it saves writing code to pick apart the Problem Number to get at the information contained inside it.

Once having established this model, you can build the database, prepare the requested report programs, and start entering the data. This can be accomplished regardless of which Problem Number conventions have been observed in the past. The given mission has been accomplished.

In addition, an investigation of the Problem Number assignment conventions now becomes feasible. For a start, you can examine a printout of the table.

As a modeling problem, the above example is not particularly interesting. Nonetheless, this "almost regular encoding" situation occurs frequently in paper-based systems, and can cause amazing amounts of trouble in conversion to an automated system. If you don't anticipate the irregularities that turn up, the complexity of all the past manually established conventions is likely to result in complexity in the code of the new automated system.

4.7.4 A Rule of Correct Attribution

Third Rule: When an object has a compound identifier—that is, one made up of two or more attributes—be sure that every attribute that is not part of the identifier represents a characteristic of the *entire object*, and not a characteristic of something which would be identified by only a part of the identifier.

Not OK:

```
Committee Membership
* Club member name
* Committee name
. Date term expires
. Club dues paid until
```
<--- This is an attrib-
ute of the club mem-
ber, not his or her
membership on the
committee

OK:

```
Committee Membership
* Club member name
* Committee name
. Date term expires
```

You can see the violation of the Third Rule: You only have to look at the Club Member Name column (and the treasurer's book) to find out what to write in the "Club dues paid until" column.   Part of the identifier is irrelevant!

The database wizard uses a slightly different vocabulary (*key* for "identifier," *primary key* for "selected identifier"—the one marked with an asterisk), and expresses the Third Rule as:

> Every non-key attribute must be fully functionally dependent on the primary key.

If an information model conforms to the first three normalization rules, you can say that the model is in Second Normal Form.

4.7.5 Another Rule of Attribution

Fourth Rule: Each attribute that is not part of an identifier must represent a characteristic of the instance named by the identifier and not a characteristic of some other non-identifier attribute.

The intention of the fourth rule is to prevent the following structure:

Not OK:

```
Salesman
* Salesman name
. Office assigned to
. Office address
```

<-- NO.   This is a characteristic of the office, which is in turn a characteristic of the salesman.

You know that you have violated the fourth rule when you see that you can fill in the "office address" value just by looking at the "office assigned to" column (and the company phonebook, for example). Since you don't need to know the salesman's name to fill in the office address, office address cannot be an attribute of Salesman.

To correct the error, split the object:

OK:

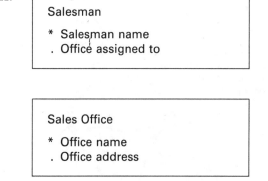

```
Salesman

 *  Salesman name
 .  Office assigned to
```

```
Sales Office

 *  Office name
 .  Office address
```

With the corrected solution, it is now possible to have a sales office that has no salesman. In the first (Not OK) solution, we would have lost all record of a sales office if we fired the last salesman assigned there.

Our database wizard states the fourth rule as:

Every non-key attribute is non-transitively dependent on the primary key.

Chapter   5

Relationships

In constructing an information model, we are concerned with identifying associations between things in the real world and reflecting those associations as precisely stated *relationships* in our model.   This chapter is concerned with characterizing binary relationships—those in which entities of two different kinds participate. Ternary and higher-order relationships will be discussed in Chapter 6.

5.1 The Concept of a Relationship

A *relationship* is the abstraction of a set of associations that hold systematically between different kinds of things in the real world:

Person LIVES IN Apartment

Library CONTAINS Book

Tenant RENTS Apartment

Satellite TRAVELS IN Orbit

The relationship is stated in terms of the formal objects that model the real-world entities participating in the association.   The capitalized words used in the examples above are considered to be the "names" of the relationships depicted.

Most relationships can also be stated in an "inverse" sense:

Dog Owner OWNS Dog
Dog IS OWNED BY Dog Owner

We think of this pair as a *single* relationship viewed from the perspective of each of the objects participating in it.

(one relationship)

For some relationships, the statement, in English, of the inverse relationship is the same as the original statement of the relationship.

Train IS NEXT TO Passenger Platform
Passenger Platform IS NEXT TO Train

Some relationships involve only one object.

Dancer IS NEXT TO Dancer.

There can be a number of different relationships between the same two objects.

> Part IS OBTAINABLE FROM Supplier
> Part IS ON ORDER FROM Supplier

One object can participate in a number of different relationships involving different objects:

> Diskette WAS FORMATTED ON Disk Drive
> Diskette IS OWNED BY Person
> Diskette CONTAINS Files

5.2 FORMS OF BINARY RELATIONSHIPS

Relationships involving only two objects can be classified into three fundamental forms, depending on the number of instances of the objects that participate in each instance of the relationship.

In other words, some relationships are . . .

> one-to-one: State HAS A Governer
> one-to-many: Dog Owner OWNS Dogs
> many-to-many: Authors WRITE Books

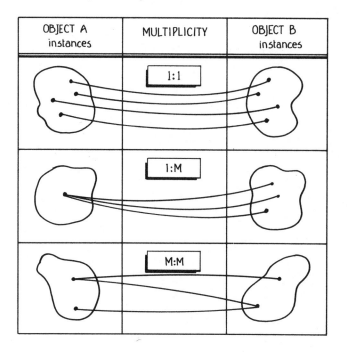

OBJECT A instances	MULTIPLICITY	OBJECT B instances
	1:1	
	1:M	
	M:M	

The terms "one-to-one," "one-to-many," and "many-to-many" are statements of the *multiplicity* of a relationship. Note that some authors use the term *cardinality* for this concept. (However, other authors use cardinality to refer to something else entirely, so we have elected to abandon this term—it's an abused word.)

We can represent these associations graphically by using boxes for the objects and arrows for the relationships. Note that the tail of the arrow always leads away from *one* instance of one of the objects, while the arrowhead points to one (single arrowhead) or many (double arrowhead) instances of the associated object.

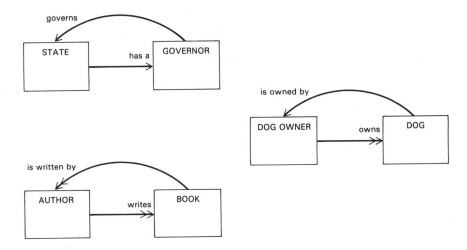

To reduce the number of lines on the page, you can combine the two relationship arrows.

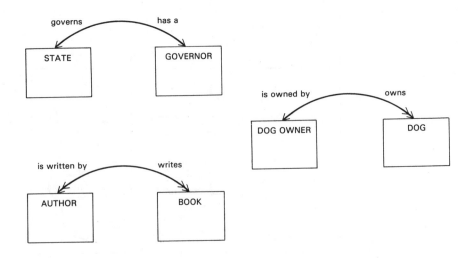

5.3 UNCONDITIONAL ONE-TO-ONE RELATIONSHIPS

5.3.1 The (1:1) Concept

In a one-to-one relationship, a given instance of a type A object is associated with one and only one instance of a type B object. Furthermore, every instance of the type B object must have an instance of the type A object so associated. This form of relationship is indicated by the symbol (1:1). In mathematical language, a one-to-one relationship is a mapping which is one-to-one and onto. This suggests the following sketch.

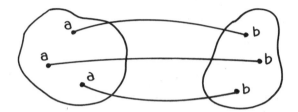

Note that the set of instances of the A object is completely *covered* by the mapping, as is the set of instances of the B object.

A real-world association which has this pattern is:

State HAS A Governor   (1:1)

where State is the Type A object and Governor is the Type B object. We can represent this relationship by:

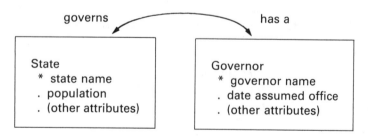

The single-pointed arrowheads are used to indicate the "one-to-oneness" of the relationship.

How do we know that this is a one-to-one relationship? A given state has exactly one governor, elected or acting, at any particular time (because that is how the laws in all the states work); a given person can be the governor of only one state at any time (again, because of law: The governor has to be a resident of the state he governs and he can be a resident of only one state at a time).

5.3.2 Modeling a (1:1) Relationship

To model a one-to-one relationship, you take an identifier

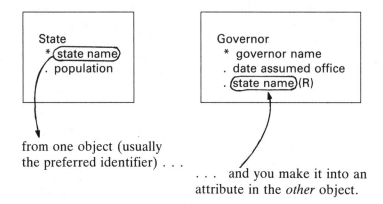

from one object (usually
the preferred identifier) . . .

. . . and you make it into an
attribute in the *other* object.

We call this attribute a *foreign key*, meaning that it is a key (identifier) for a table other than the one in which it appears. Note that the new attribute is referential. This fact is indicated on the graphic by the (R) appended to the attribute name.

To model a one-to-one relationship, the foreign key may be placed in either of the tables. Hence, instead, we could have made an attribute State.Governor Name.

Returning, however, to the formulation using the attribute Governor.State Name, we have a new task. Since we have defined this additional attribute, we will have to provide an attribute description and a statement of the domain of this new attribute. Since the domain of Governor.State Name is *necessarily* the same as that of State.State Name, we just say so:

> *Attribute:* Governor.State Name
> *Description:* The state which is governed by this governor.
> *Domain:* Same as State.State Name

When we describe the domain of a referential attribute in this way, we are saying that the only legal values for Governor.State Name are values that are *actually taken on* by State.State Name. Values that might be permitted for State.State Name at some other point in time are not permitted for Governor.State Name. So, for example, the attribute description for State.State Name (a naming attribute) would certainly permit the creation of states with names like Puerto Rico, West Kentucky, or Orefornia; however, one is not allowed to consider a governor of

Orefornia until such a state has been created. In other words, domains for referential attributes are specified by extension, whereas domains for non-referential attributes are specified by intension.

Finally, we note that the definition of the relationship imposes certain requirements, known as *integrity constraints*, to ensure that the data in the system is consistent with the model and consistent with itself. The integrity constraints arising from a one-to-one unconditional relationship, stated in terms of the example given above, require any implementation based on this model to account for the following:

1. If a state (or governor) is to be removed from the system, the corresponding governor (or state) must also be removed. These must happen as a single operation in order to leave the data consistent with the model.
2. If a state (or governor) is to be added to the system, the corresponding governor (or state) must be added simultaneously.

5.4 UNCONDITIONAL ONE-TO-MANY RELATIONSHIPS

5.4.1 The (1:M) Concept

In an unconditional one-to-many relationship, denoted by the symbol (1:M), a single instance of a type A object is associated with one or more instances of a type B object. Every instance of the type B object is associated with exactly one instance of the type A object. The schematic association has this pattern:

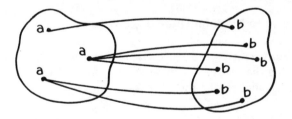

Again, note that all instances of both objects participate in the mapping. For example:

Department IS STAFFED BY Employees (1:M)

The sketch corresponding to this particular relationship is as follows. Again, note the convention of the double arrowhead: It points to the "many" object.

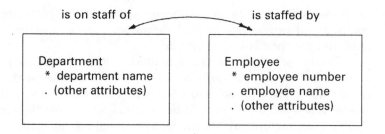

How do we know this is a one-to-many relationship? Our evidence must come from statements of terminology and policy for the company being modeled. In this example, we presume that these statements say that a single department has a staff made up of a number of employees, that a given employee is considered to be on the staff of only one department at a time, and that every employee must be assigned to a department.

Since "many" is defined as "one or more," our relationship statement covers the case of one-person departments. Note that the case of an unstaffed (zero employees) department is *not* covered. If the organization that we are modeling considered that to be a valid concept, we would not be able to use this relationship form to reflect the situation.

Additional examples:

> Dog Owner OWNS Dogs (1:M)
> Airplane IS POWERED BY Engines (1:M)
> Insurance Client OWNS Policies (1:M)
> Substation CONTAINS Circuit Breakers (1:M)

5.4.2 How to Model a One-to-Many Relationship

Let us start with two objects, Substation and Circuit Breaker. The real-world situation is that every circuit breaker is located in a substation, and a substation contains a number of circuit breakers.

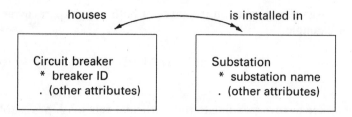

Again, we make the relationship precise by developing an appropriate additional attribute. In this case, we take an identifier from the "many object"—

the circuit breaker—and make a new attribute in the "one object"—the substation. The new attribute is referential in nature.

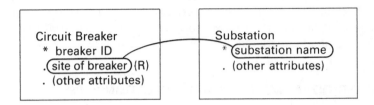

Note that the new attribute can have a name different from that of the name of the attribute from which it is derived. In general, we try to name these referential (relationship-implementing) attributes by the role they are playing in the object in which they are placed: hence, site of breaker.We must now describe the new attribute and its domain:

> *Attribute:* Circuit Breaker.Site of Breaker
> *Description:* The substation in which the circuit breaker is installed.
> *Domain:* Same as Substation.Substation Name

The integrity constraint that is imposed by this relationship is similar to that from the one-to-one case: The collection of values of Circuit Breaker.Site of Breaker *must be the same* as the collection of values of Substation.Substation Name. That is, it will not be legal to have a configuration where there is a Circuit Breaker sited at a Substation that does not appear in the substation table or where there is a Substation that contains no circuit breakers, according to the Circuit Breaker table. An implementation based upon this model must, therefore, make provisions to ensure this level of consistency. In particular, the following cases must be accounted for:

1. A substation may not be deleted from the Substation table if that would cause circuit breakers in the Circuit Breaker table to be stranded without a substation. If a substation is to be deleted, its resident circuit breakers must also be deleted in the same operation.
2. A circuit breaker may not be deleted from the Circuit Breaker table if that would cause a substation to be left unpopulated by breakers. This would violate the definition of substation.
3. A new circuit breaker can, of course, be added if it is sited at an existing substation. However, if the substation is not already present, *both the substation and at least one new circuit breaker* must be added simultaneously.

Similarly, when a new substation is added, at least one circuit breaker must be added to populate the substation.

Finally, a thinking problem: In the case of the state/governor example in the last section, we saw that there were two ways to model the one-to-one relationship that holds between those two objects. Convince yourself that this is *not* the case for the one-to-many relationship of this example.

5.5 UNCONDITIONAL MANY-TO-MANY RELATIONSHIPS

5.5.1 The (M:M) Concept

In a many-to-many relationship, denoted by the symbol (M:M), every instance of the type A object is associated with one or more instances of the type B object, and every instance of the type B object is associated with one or more instances of type A. Schematically, we have:

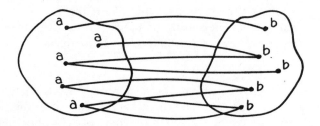

In an (unconditional) many-to-many relationship, all instances of both objects are covered by the mapping.

An example of a many-to-many relationship is

Novel WAS WRITTEN BY Author (M:M)

The many-to-many case is depicted as follows. Again, note the arrowhead convention.

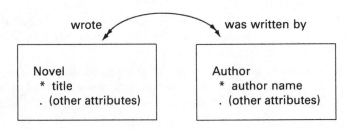

By modeling this association as a many-to-many relationship, we have reflected the real-world situation, allowing for (1) multiple novels by a single author and (2) the possibility of two or more authors collaborating on a single novel. We have also eliminated the possibility of a novel that has no author (presumably, we agreed to include Anonymous as an author in our world).

Note that we have also done something fairly questionable in this model fragment: We have eliminated the possibility of calling someone an Author who has not produced at least one Novel. There are two possible explanations for this.

1. What is the definition of the Author object? We would have to look at the object description to determine this, but it is possible that Author is *defined* as a Novel writer (as opposed to a biographer, for example).

2. What is the problem domain of this model fragment? If it involves a small lending library operated as a sideline to a beauty shop, for example, the model is likely to be correct: The lending library, by policy of the owners of the beauty shop, stocks only novels.

   On the other hand, if we are talking about a general public library or a bookseller's world, and if we consider someone who has written any kind of book to be an author, the model is not accurate in its present form. Some other relationship form would be required to capture the association existing between novels and authors, since there can be authors who have never written a novel.

The above discussion has taken us away from our original target, the basic many-to-many relationship. However, it has served to illustrate the significance of the assertion that the details of any particular model depend upon the reality being modeled. It is simply not possible to evaluate the correctness of a model without comparing it to the reality it is trying to reflect!

Here are a few more examples of many-to-many relationships. As a thinking problem, try to imagine a problem domain in which these are valid many-to-many relationships. What constitutes an appropriate object description for each object?

> Record Set CONTAINS Composition (M:M)
> Flight LANDS AT Airport (M:M)
> Part IS A COMPONENT OF Machine (M:M)

5.5.2 How to Model a (M:M) Relationship

Now suppose we want to model a many-to-many relationship such as Part IS COMPONENT OF Appliance.

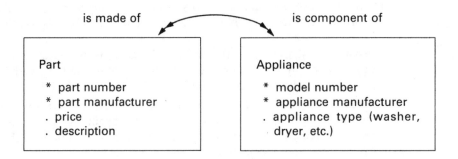

To do this, we make up a special table from the identifiers of each object:

COMPOSITION

Part Number	Part Manufacturer	Model Number	Appliance Manufacturer
103	GE	176A	GE
103	GE	92AB	Maytag
21	Sears	12345	Sears
986	Radio Shack	12345	Sears

We call this construction a *correlation table*, because it is needed to record the relationship, or correlation, between two other objects in the model. The correlation table is drawn as shown below:

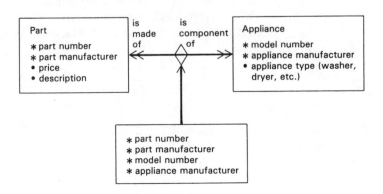

5.6 SEMANTICS AND MODELING OF CONDITIONAL FORMS

Conditional relationships, of which there are seven forms, are derived from the unconditional forms which were discussed earlier in this chapter. The only difference is that in an unconditional relationship every instance of each object participates; in a conditional relationship there may be instances which do not participate.

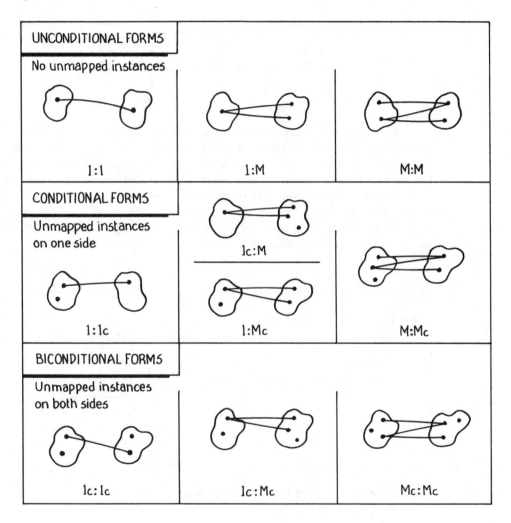

5.6.1 How to Model a One-to-One Conditional Relationship (1:1c)

A one-to-one conditional relationship, denoted by the symbol (1:1c), is just like a one-to-one unconditional relationship, except that all instances of *one* of the objects need not participate in the relationship. Note that one of the objects participating in the relationship is covered by the mapping, but the other is not.

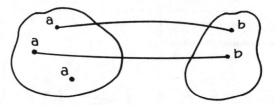

An example of such a relationship is Senator FILLS Senate Seat. Senate seats always exist—there are always one hundred in the U.S. Senate—but at any given time, all seats need not be filled (death of a senator or disputed election). On the other hand, no person is a Senator unless that person occupies a seat.

A one-to-one conditional relationship is modeled by adding a referential attribute to the object which always participates (the Senator, in the above example) in the relationship. The additional attribute is a foreign key to the other object, just as with an ordinary unconditional one-to-one relationship.

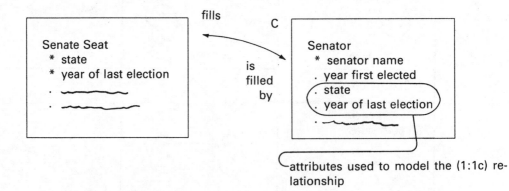

attributes used to model the (1:1c) relationship

5.6.2 How to Model a One-to-One Biconditional Relationship (1c:1c)

In a one-to-one biconditional relationship, denoted by (1c:1c), one instance of the type A object is associated with zero or one instance of the type B object. Furthermore, one instance of the type B object is associated with zero or one instance of type A.

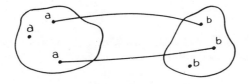

Example:

Consider two objects PLUG and SOCKET. There is a relationship: Plug IS PLUGGED INTO Socket. Instances of each object can exist which do not participate in the IS PLUGGED INTO relationship.

There are two ways to model a one-to-one biconditional relationship.

1. Foreign key: Here you choose one of the objects (for example, Plug), and add an attribute that is a foreign key to the other object (Socket plugged into), just like in a one-to-one unconditional relationship. This method is usually very easy to comprehend, but has the disadvantage that it leads to a number of "not connected" values in the table, should one construct a stored data scheme that is based directly on the information model.

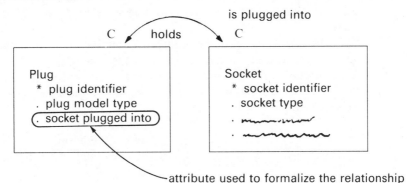

2. Correlation table: In this formulation, you make a correlation table ("Connections" would be an appropriate name) that records only those instances of plugs and sockets which are connected. The instances which do not participate in the relationship are simply omitted.

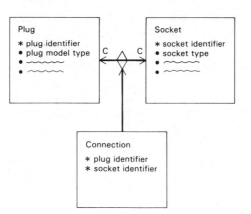

5.6.3 How to Model a One-to-Many Conditional (on the "one" side) Relationship (1c:M)

A one-to-many conditional relationship, denoted by (1c:M), has the following properties:

- Each instance of the type A object is associated with one or more of the type B objects. Every instance of type A participates in the relationship.
- An instance of the type B object is associated with one or zero type A objects; that is, not all instances of type B participate.

Example

> United States Citizen WAS BORN IN State
> State IS BIRTHPLACE OF United States Citizen

Each state is the birthplace of a number of United States citizens; in addition, there are also United States citizens who were born outside of the United States of America.

The (1c:M) form can be modeled by adding an attribute to the object on the "many" side (United States Citizen, in the example above) of the relationship. This attribute will sometimes have null ("born on foreign soil") values. Using now the textual notation for an object with its attributes, and underlining the preferred identifiers, we have:

> State (state name, date of statehood, ...)
> United States Citizen (name, state of birth, birth year ...)

attribute used to model the relationship

Alternatively, one can construct a correlation table.

5.6.4 How to Model a One-to-Many Conditional (on the "many" side) Relationship (1:Mc)

This form of relationship is conditional on the "many" side: Each instance of the type A object is associated with zero or more instances of type B, while each instance of type B is associated with exactly one instance of type A.

As an illustration of this form of relationship, consider Tax Return and Dependent. Each Tax Return claims zero, one, or more Dependents; while each Dependent is claimed on exactly one Tax Return. The last condition is ensured by the tax law which requires that more than 50% of the cost of support of a Dependent be paid by the (filer of the) Tax Return. Note that the object Tax

Return refers to a single tax return which may, of course, be signed by several individuals.

This relationship form may be modeled by adding an attribute to the "many" (Dependent) side.

Tax Return (<u>first taxpayer ID number</u>, name, address, ...)
Dependent (<u>dependent name</u>, <u>tax return claimed on</u>, ...)

attribute used to model the (1:Mc) relationship.

Domain: Same as Tax Return. First Taxpayer ID Number

Note that in this particular example, the attribute Dependent.Tax Return Claimed On is serving two functions: It is part of the primary key of Dependent *and* it is formalizing the relationship Dependent CLAIMED ON Tax Return.

5.6.5 How to Model a One-to-Many Biconditional Relationship (1c:Mc)

This is a form of the basic one-to-many relationship, but there can be instances of both types of objects which do not participate in the relationship. As an example, consider the case: Office IS ASSIGNED TO Employees.

- An office may be assigned to one or more employees.
- There can be offices which are currently assigned to no one.
- There can be employees, whose jobs do not involve office work, who are not assigned office space.

This relationship form can be modeled by adding an attribute to the object on the "many side" (Employee.Office number, for instance), in which case there will be null values required for those instances of the many-object which don't participate. If there are a lot of non-participating instances, you might prefer to construct a correlation table, recording only those instances that do participate.

5.6.6 How to Model a Many-to-Many Conditional Relationship (M:Mc)

The many-to-many conditional relationship is just like the ordinary unconditional (M:M) relationship, except that instances of one of the objects can exist which do not participate in the relationship.

For example, consider the relationship, Member SERVES ON Committee:

- A single club member is permitted to serve on multiple committees at the same time.
- An individual club member is permitted to serve on no committee at all.
- More than one member, almost by definition of the word "committee", is allowed to work on a given committee. Since "one" is considered to be a special case of "many", the case of a one-person committee is also covered.

Like other many-to-many relationships, (M:Mc) is modeled by constructing a correlation table that records only those instances of the objects that participate in the relationship.

Committee Membership (<u>club member</u> name, <u>committee</u> name)

                                ↑   ↑

                             Domain: Domain:

                             Same as   Same as

                             Member.Name   Committee.Name

5.6.7 How to Model a Many-to-Many Biconditional Relationship (Mc:Mc)

The many-to-many biconditional relationship resembles the basic many-to-many unconditional form, except there can be instances of both objects that do not participate in the relationship.

At the beginning of the semester at a university, classes are scheduled and students are invited to sign up. Until the end of the registration period, classes can be listed which have no students registered in them. Furthermore, depending on university rules, there can be some individuals who have official student status, but are registered for no classes at all (perhaps such a student is working on a thesis).

During the registration period, the relationship Student IS REGISTERED FOR Class is a many-to-many biconditional relationship. (Of course, after the end of registration, the classes for which no students are registered are deleted from the schedule, and the relationship is converted to the (M:Mc) form).

As with other many-to-many relationships, (Mc:Mc) is modeled by a correlation table.

Chapter   6

Constructions Involving Many Objects

6.1 SUBTYPES AND SUPERTYPES

Let us suppose that we have several classes of things in the real world. The classes are truly distinct, leading us to model each class as a separate object. At the same time, the real world instances that make up the classes are significantly similar, and one would like to capture that fact in the model. How do you do it? The following example shows how.

Let us start with the separate objects. The Substation and Gap Breaker Station objects model real world units in the electrical power distribution system for a mass transit authority. The attributes with the word "indication" in their names reflect sensor-based data which can be monitored in real time.

```
SUBSTATION                          GAP BREAKER STATION
* substation ID                     * gap breaker station ID
· local/remote indication           · local/remote indication
· control power                     · control power
  ok/not ok indication                ok/not ok indication
· transformer fault                 · cubicle trouble
  indication                          indication
```

Now we take all the attributes that are common to all of the separate objects—the *subtype objects*—and use these attributes as the basis for generalizing a new object, which we call the *supertype object*.

> ELECTRIFICATION STATION
> * electrification station ID
> · local/remote indication
> · control power ok/not ok
>   indication

Next, we go to the original set of objects from which we generalized the supertype, and remove all the non-identifier attributes which duplicate those assigned to the supertype.

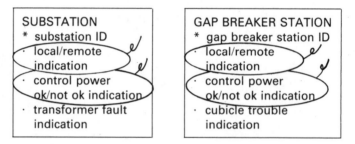

> SUBSTATION
> * substation ID
> · local/remote indication
> · control power ok/not ok indication
> · transformer fault indication

> GAP BREAKER STATION
> * gap breaker station ID
> · local/remote indication
> · control power ok/not ok indication
> · cubicle trouble indication

Now, how do we draw the relationship between our supertype object and the subtype objects from which it was abstracted? We already know one way:

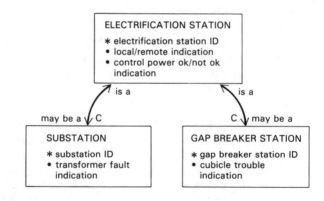

> ELECTRIFICATION STATION
> * electrification station ID
> • local/remote indication
> • control power ok/not ok indication

is a   is a

may be a C   C may be a

> SUBSTATION
> * substation ID
> • transformer fault indication

> GAP BREAKER STATION
> * gap breaker station ID
> • cubicle trouble indication

Note, however, that this drawing does not tell the whole story: It does not say that every Electrification Station *must be either* a Substation or a Gap Breaker Station. A special drawing convention is used to note this fact:

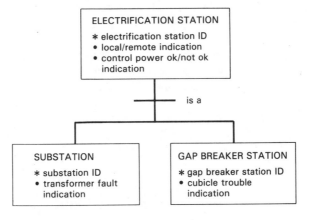

The relationship between the subtype objects and their supertype is noted on the drawing as "must be exactly one of" or, more concisely, "is a."

How do we express subtype/supertype relationship in terms of attributes? There are basically two cases to consider.

1. If you already have identifiers of the subtype objects and *their domains are disjoint,* you can create an identifier for the supertype object from the identifiers for each of the subtypes.

Attribute: Electrification Station ID
Domain: Same as the union of the domains of Gap Breaker Station.Gap Breaker Station ID and Substation.Substation ID

2. If the domains of the subtype identifiers are *not disjoint* (for example, both substations and gap breaker stations were identified with numbers assigned starting at 1), this won't work, since the supertype (Electrification Station) instances would not be uniquely identified.   Here you have a choice:

    (a) Create new arbitrary identifiers for each of the subtype objects (for example, by prefixing "S" to the previously given identifier of a substation, and "G" to the previously given identifier of each gap breaker station).   Now you have disjoint domains for the subtype identifiers, so you can proceed as in 1 above.

    (b) Create a compound identifier for the supertype object, by using the given non-disjoint identifiers of the subtypes together with an additional Type attribute.   For the example we have been using,

Attribute: Electrification Station.Electrification Station ID

Domain: Same as the union of the domains of Gap Breaker Station.Gap
Breaker Station ID and Substation.Substation ID.

Attribute: Electrification Station.Type
Domain: [substation|gap breaker station]

The subtype/supertype concept can be drawn on repeatedly in the same problem,
as shown below. Note especially that some of the objects participate in more than
one subtype/supertype structure.

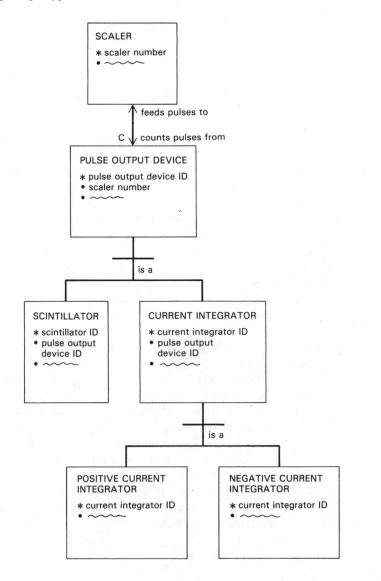

Problem (Electronic Parts Storage).   Our problem is to keep track of electronic parts used by a company that specializes in custom, low volume fabrication orders.   The company has arranged its parts according to the set of rules given below.   Construct a model which expresses the rules and allows you to answer the question "where would I look to find an XYZ chip, if we have any?"

1. There are a large number of separately identifiable *bins*, each about the size of a coffee mug.

2. Every bin contains some number of identical electronic parts (chips, for instance).   We don't care how many chips are in each bin.

3. For convenience, the bins can be placed on *trays*.   Every tray has been assigned an identification number, which is conspicuously painted on it.

4. Trays can be carried around easily, whether or not there are any bins on the trays.

5. There are a number of *workrooms*, each containing some number of *cabinets*.

6. Trays can be inserted in *cabinets*.

7. A tray can be placed on a workbench or anywhere else in one of the workrooms.   The workbenches are not separately identified (they don't have any names or numbers and, because of the crowded furniture arrangement, it is not easy to say where one begins or ends).

8. From time to time, we rearrange the furniture in the workrooms, and sometimes we move a cabinet from one workroom to another.

6.2 ASSOCIATIVE OBJECTS

6.2.1 Concept of an Associative Object

An associative object arises when there is supplementary information associated with instances of a relationship.   Here is an example.

Let us suppose that we have a specification object Drug, representing drugs which are approved for clinical use by the appropriate governmental agency.   In addition, we have a Drug Manufacturer object, representing enterprises which are capable of manufacturing the drugs of interest, and a many-to-many conditional relationship Drug Manufacturer IS LICENSED TO MANUFACTURE Drug (Mc:M).

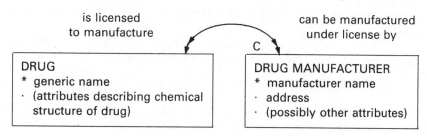

From Chapter 5, we know that the relationship can be modeled by means of a correlation table which contains generic drug name and manufacturer name attributes.

Generic name	Manufacturer name
aspirin	Acme Drugs, Ltd.
diazepem	Zenith Pharmaceuticals
aspirin	Zenith Pharmaceuticals

There is more that can be said about this association between drugs and drug manufacturers: the date the license was issued, for example. This leads us to the following construct:

```
LICENSE
 * manufacturer name
 * generic drug name
 · date licensed
```

You can think of the many-to-many relationship with which we started as having been converted to two one-to-many relationships, each involving the intermediate associative object (License) which was developed by augmenting the correlation table. In terms of the graphical representation tools we have so far, this would be expressed as:

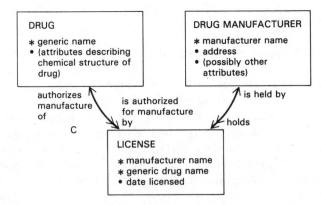

but a more expressive graphical representation will be provided in the following section.

Now, how should we name the relationship(s) in which the License object participates? First, remember that we started with:

Drug Manufacturer IS LICENSED TO MANUFACTURE Drug (Mc:M).

Looking at Drug, Drug Manufacturer, and License (as an object), we could recast this relationship to bring out the role of the License:

License IS AN AUTHORIZATION FOR MANUFACTURE OF Drug BY Drug Manufacturer.

Note that this can always be done with an associative object involving two other objects: You get a 3-object relationship statement that has the form "⟨associative object⟩ IS A ⟨PHRASE⟩ ⟨object 1⟩ . . . ⟨object 2⟩."

6.2.2 Single-Occurrence Form

The preceding example illustrates what we call the "single occurrence form": One instance of the associative object (License) is associated with a single pairing of the two original objects (Drug and Drug Manufacturer). The symbol we use to denote this situation is:

$$1\text{-}\langle rel \rangle$$

where ⟨rel⟩ is replaced by the symbol for the original underlying relationship. Hence, for the relationship in the example above, we write:

License IS AN AUTHORIZATION FOR MANUFACTURE OF Drug BY Drug Manufacturer 1-(M:Mc)

because the License object is based on the correlation table generated by our original relationship:

Drug Manufacturer IS LICENSED TO MANUFACTURE Drug (Mc:M).

The "one associative instance per associated pair" property is a fundamental aspect of the reality we reflect in our information model. The graphical representation we use to bring out this fact is the following:

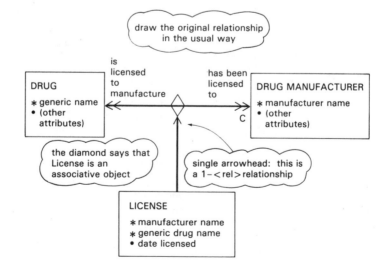

6.2.3 Multiple Occurrence Form

Extending the previous example, consider the Batch object:

```
BATCH
*  manufacturer name
*  generic drug name
*  batch number
·  date of manufacture
·  quality control status
```

Like License, Batch is an associative object reflecting a relationship between Drug Manufacturer and Drug:

Drug Manufacturer MANUFACTURES Drug (Mc:M).

This situation is quite different, however, because there can be *any number* of batches associated with a given drug/drug manufacturer combination. This form— "many associative instances per associated pair"—is symbolized **M - ⟨rel⟩** where, as before, we substitute for ⟨rel⟩ the underlying relationship form between the non-associative objects. Hence, for our example, we would write:

Batch IS A MANUFACTURING OF Drug BY Manufacturer M-(M:Mc).

The graphical representation for this form is:

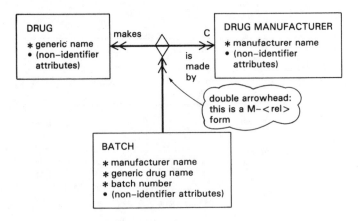

Problem.   Construct an information model that permits the illegal manufacture of drugs (Drug Manufacturer makes Batches of Drugs, whether or not he has a License to do so).

Problem.   Construct a model that allows the Drug Manufacturer to make Batches of only those Drugs for which he holds a License.

6.2.4 More on Associative Objects

Associative Object vs. Correlation Table.   Is there any real difference between an associative object and a correlation table?   Consider again the drug licensing example. If we model the relationship Drug Manufacturer IS LICENSED TO MAKE Drug (Mc:M) as:

Drug Manufacturer	Drug

without reference to a license entity, we would call it a "correlation table", since there are no attributes other than the identifiers from the Drug and Drug Manufacturer objects.   The only information contained in this table is the correlation or association between the instances participating in the relationship.   This construction would be depicted graphically as:

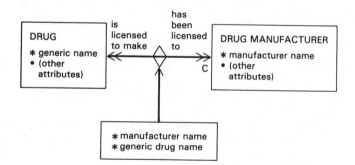

If, on the other hand, we focus on License as an object, a different construction seems to emerge.   First, it is proper to assume that each license can be identified by a license number—if the license-issuing agency doesn't do this already, it certainly could do so.   Secondly, License has plausible descriptive attributes: License.Date of Issue and License.Expiration Date.   There is little doubt that License is a well-defined object in its own right.

So now we have three objects to correlate: License, Drug, and Drug Manufacturer. This leads one to a symmetric graphic rendition, which treats each object equally and makes use of a three-object correlation table. Note the single arrow leading to the diamond from the correlation table: This indicates that there is one correlation for each instance of the three-object relationship.

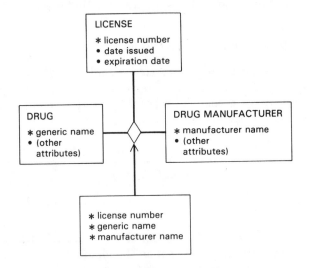

Compare this to the asymmetric construction given in Section 6.2.2. Examination of the attributes in the two models reveals that the asymmetric construction can be derived from the symmetric form by merging (actually "joining," to use the proper database term) the correlation table with the License object and removing the attribute License.License Number.

Given that we now have two forms which can be used to express the same set of real-world facts, which should we choose? Our current preference is for the asymmetric form, since it depicts more clearly the form of the relationship (the number of legal combinations of the participating instances).

Four or More Objects.   The symmetric form discussed above has one stunning advantage: It can be extended to cope with a relationship which necessarily involves four or more objects. This is potentially very useful. Because of the number of different possibilities for relationship forms when four or more objects are involved, we have not yet attempted to develop a classification system akin to that for the three-object associations 1 - ⟨rel⟩ and M - ⟨rel⟩.

Note that relationships involving four or more objects rarely arise in practice—in fact, they are so rare that we don't have a totally defensible example to share. However, should you find yourself having to deal with such a relationship, we suggest that you draw it like this.

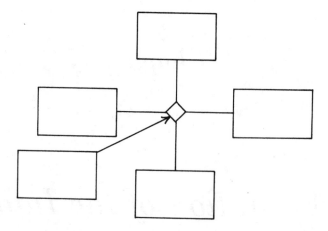

In addition, it would seem prudent to document any such relationship in some detail, to state clearly any integrity constraints which must be placed on the model.

Chapter   7

Representation of the Information Model

Good, practical forms of documentation are necessary to keep the reader—and the writer—from getting overwhelmed.   This chapter presents several graphical and textual document forms which we have found useful and effective.

There are two graphical forms:

- Information Structure Diagram
- Overview Information Structure Diagram

and three textual forms:

- Object Specification Document
- Relationship Specification Document
- Summary Specification

The information model representations presented here should be regarded as well-tested suggestions.   You may find it necessary to make minor adaptations, particularly if you are using a computer-aided drawing program or a CASE (computer-aided software engineering) tool.   For example, some CASE tools place a diamond on the relationship connection, whether or not an associative object is involved; some use @ where we use an asterisk.   This kind of variation in notation is clearly insignificant.   On the other hand, if you can't define associative objects or subtype/supertype constructions, you should probably look for better tools.

7.1 INFORMATION STRUCTURE DIAGRAM

The Information Structure Diagram is based on various forms of Entity Relationship Diagrams used over the past few years [Tsiritzis and Lochovsky, 1982; Martin, 1985; Chen, 1977].   The Information Structure Diagram is concerned only with *declaring* the objects, attributes, and relationships of the model.   Because it does not present their meaning, it cannot be said to define these elements.

The Information Structure Diagram contains a great deal of information: One might expect it to become unmanageable with large scale problems.   We have found this to be true in part.   Nevertheless, we continue to rely upon this form, since various attempts to simplify it have not stood up in practice.

The symbols used in the Information Structure Diagram were introduced in Chapters 3 through 6, and are summarized here for convenience.

An object together with its attributes is shown by a box.   The attributes may be annotated to show their usage in the model:

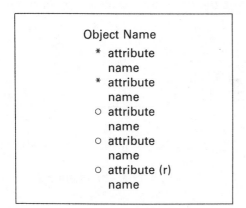

Prefix any attribute which is part of the preferred identifier with an asterisk.

Prefix an attribute which is not a part of the preferred identifier with a dot or circle.

Append an (r) to any attribute which is used to formalize a relationship.

The attributes may be listed in any order.

Binary relationships are declared by arrows drawn between the object boxes.

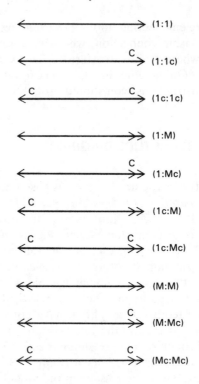

The line representing the relationship is annotated with the name of the relationship, stated from the point of view of both participating objects. The verb phrase for each point of view is placed on the end of the arrow that points to the object of the sentence. For example:

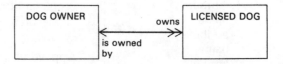

can be read "Dog Owner OWNS Licensed Dog," or "Licensed Dog IS OWNED BY Dog Owner."

A conditional relationship has a 'C' placed near the relationship phrase that is sometimes true. For example:

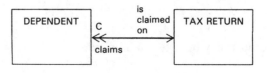

This relationship can be read "Dependent IS CLAIMED ON Tax Return" and "Tax Return (MAY) CLAIM Dependents." Note that the marker to show that the relationship is conditional is placed by the relationship phrase that is sometimes true.

When a correlation table is used to model a relationship, it is drawn as:

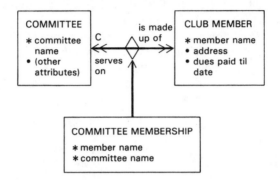

When an associative object arises from a relationship, a diamond is placed on the line representing the relationship, and the associative object is connected to the diamond. The relationship line is one of the forms defined above.

The associative object may have one or two arrowheads pointing to the diamond. A single arrowhead indicates that a single instance of the associative object may exist for each instance of the association; a double arrowhead indicates that many instances of the associative object can exist for each instance of the association.

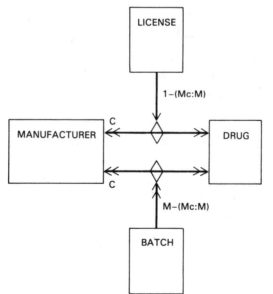

A *single* license is issued for each legal manufacturer of the drug, but *many* batches of the drug can be made by each manufacturer.

We have also found it useful to have notation to denote the case that *all* instances of one object must be related to *all* instances of another object. Consider, for example, a billing system in which the objects Service Period and Billing Group are defined. A Service Period is defined as a time during which a service is provided, for example one month. A Billing Group is a set of accounts all billed as a unit in a single run. Each account is placed in a single billing group, and every group must be billed in every month. This leads to a many-to-many-all relationship between Service Period and Billing Group which we show graphically as:

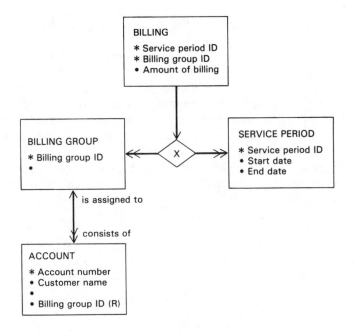

A subtype/supertype construction is drawn as:

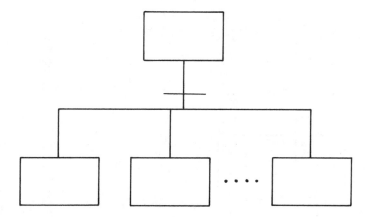

The small bar indicates which object is the supertype object. All the other objects so connected are subtype objects.

If you number the objects and relationships on the Information Structure Diagram, the diagram can serve as a "graphic table of contents" to the more detailed textual Object and Relationship Specification documents.

Typically, the detailed graphical representation of the model will not fit on an 8.5 x 11-inch page. One solution is to divide the model into sections, placing each section on a separate page. Some objects must then be duplicated on several pages.

For a large model, it is helpful to use oversized pages. The large paper typically used to produce engineering drawings in a drafting department is sometimes just the thing. If you aren't familiar with this old-fashioned pencil and eraser technology, we suggest that you consult a neighboring architect, engineer, or draftsman; or stop by a convenient graphics supply shop.

A pitfall to avoid: The Information Structure Diagram contains so much information that one is sometimes tempted to rely on it entirely, omitting the Object and Relationship Specification documents. Doing so undermines the central purpose of the Information Model. It is equivalent to printing a dictionary without the meaning of the words!

7.2 THE OVERVIEW INFORMATION STRUCTURE DIAGRAM

This representation is just like the Information Structure Diagram described previously, except that the attribute names are omitted from the boxes. This makes the picture much more manageable, but quite ambiguous in many cases. Its use is best confined to overviews, presentations, and the like.

After studying the following Overview Information Structure Diagram, turn to Appendix A and compare the overview form with the Information Structure Diagram for the same problem. This should give you some feel for the comparative scale and communication power of the two forms.

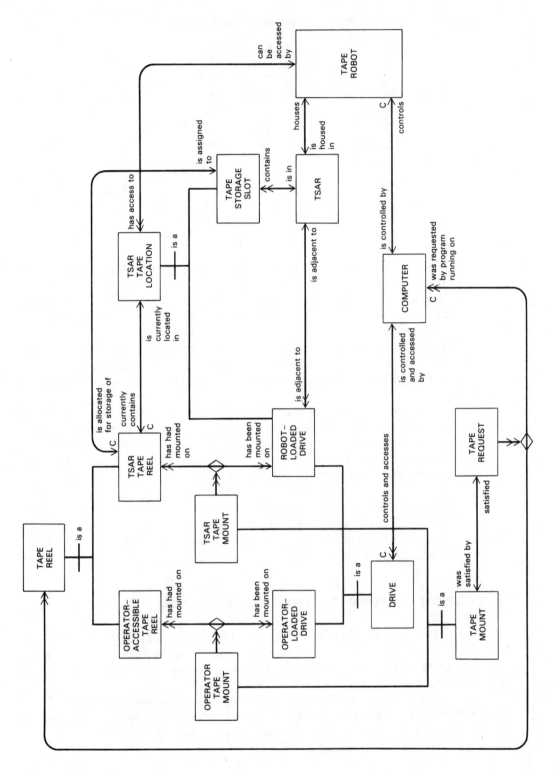

82

7.3 THE OBJECT SPECIFICATION DOCUMENT

The Object Specification document presents the entire model in text. It is intended to describe the reality being modeled—the real-world subject matter—and show how that reality has been formalized in the model. This is no mean trick! This document obviously contains a tremendous amount of information; the challenge is to find a form and organization that makes it both useable and complete.

We normally organize our Object Specification Documents in this way:

> **I.** *Table of Contents.* A listing of the objects covered in the Object Specification Document, together with their page numbers. Alternatively, one might use a "graphical table of contents": An Overview Information Structure Diagram, with each object annotated with the page number on which its specification begins.
>
> **II.** The specification for a single object, organized as follows:
>   A. The name of the object, given in a section heading.
>   B. A textual declaration of the object with its attributes. Attributes comprising the preferred identifier are underlined.
>   C. A listing of additional identifiers, if any. We have found it wise to repeat the preferred identifier, even though it is redundant, since this makes the model easier to maintain.
>   D. The object description.
>   E. A specification for each attribute of the object, organized as follows:
>   1. A section heading, one layer deeper in the section-numbering hierarchy, giving the name of the attribute to be described.
>   2. The description of that attribute.
>   3. Information about the function of the attribute in the model: If the attribute is being used to model a relationship, a statement to that effect is included.
>   4. A declaration of the domain of the attribute.
>   F. Specification of the next attribute.
>   G. Specification of the next attribute.
>   . . .
>
> **III.** Specification of the next object (start on a new page).
>
> **IV.** Specification for the next object (start on a new page).
>
> **V.** Etc.

Note that a specification is provided for *every* object in the model. Associative objects are considered objects for this purpose, but correlation tables are not.

Many minor variations on the above form work equally well. Some of these variations can be seen in the sample models in the appendices.

7.4 THE RELATIONSHIPS SPECIFICATION DOCUMENT

This document consists of a set of specifications, one for each relationship in the model.

We normally organize relationship descriptions as follows:

1. The heading consists of the name of the relationship, from the point of view of each participating object, and a statement of the multiplicity and conditionality in the short form described in section 7.1.

2. A description of the real-world association being modeled by the relationship. The description should also include statements justifying the multiplicity and conditionality of the relationship. It is all too easy to fall into mechanical statements here: "Every dog is owned, and it can have only one owner." The question, of course, is "Why?" The Dog License Bureau is only concerned with licensed dogs and *by policy* a dog is only registered to a single individual.

3. The final portion of each relationship description contains a description of how the relationship is formalized in attributes. For example: The relationship is formalized by the attribute Dog.Owner Name which refers to the Dog Owner.

   An equivalent cryptic style is:

   Formalization: Dog.Owner Name -⟩ Dog Owner

Real-world relationships, that are reflected in correlation tables or associative objects, are also included in the Relationship Specification Document.

The Relationship Specification document is sometimes combined with the Object Specification document, especially if the model is a small one.

Examples of Relationship Specifications can be found in the sample models in the appendices.

7.5 THE SUMMARY DOCUMENT

The summary specification is a short form document, which is frequently put together as a ready-reference sheet. It has this form:

--- OBJECTS ---

Region (region name, length, start address)

Common (common block name, length, start address, region)

Allocation Block (data type, element width, permitted access, common block name, index of first unused word)

Table (long table name, short table name, number of rows, number of rows in use)

Column (<u>FORTRAN</u> <u>variable</u> <u>name</u>, column name, table name, elements in data item, data type, element width, storage width, permitted access, start index)

--- RELATIONSHIPS ---

Region CONTAINS Common Block   (1:Mc)
Common Block IS CONTAINED IN Region

Common Block MAY BE AN Allocation Block   (1:1c)
Allocation Block IS A Common Block

Allocation Block STORES Column   (1:M)
Column IS STORED IN Allocation Block

Table IS COMPRISED OF Columns   (1:M)
Column IS CONTAINED IN Table

Chapter 8

Techniques

So far, we have described in some detail how to translate one's understanding of a real-world problem into the form of an Information Model. Now comes the hard part: How does one gain the necessary understanding?

It goes without saying that a good understanding of any problem is built on a great deal of expert information. This chapter presents some specific suggestions for collecting the requisite information, together with some techniques that we believe to be helpful for converting that information into understanding.

8.1 DOCUMENT RESEARCH

A great deal of information can frequently be extracted from documents that were generated by or for application experts. Obvious candidate documents include specifications for computer systems (particularly if you are doing this analysis as part of a replacement or upgrade project), work flow analyses, operational procedures manuals, and signal lists. In addition, you might look for:

Forms. Forms reveal how somebody thinks about the problem. Read both blank and completed forms, and investigate discrepancies/irregularities. Forms include such things as customer bills, charge slips, change orders, and problem reports.

Reports, hand-tabulations, spreadsheets.   Tabulations of data can also be an interesting source.   As with forms, you may find poorly factored attributes, cases of misattribution, and similar flaws.   Try to unearth the underlying assumptions.

Engineering drawings.   Schematics of various kinds, logic diagrams, construction drawings, and such are frequently a good source—particularly for questions of multiplicity and mechanism of relationship.

Miscellaneous problem-dependent items.   Operator's training materials, photographs of displays, aerial photographs, laws, information pamphlets from the post office, calibration curves and similar plotted data, and rate schedules are also good sources.

If you find that you need more general background information, of course you will remember to investigate your favorite bookstore, as well as public and university libraries.   In addition, there may be a company library that you can make use of.

8.2 DIALOG

Dialog is an ancient technique, still unsurpassed, in which thinking men seek to state valid and universally applicable definitions ("universal truths").   An effective dialog typically swings back and forth between high levels of abstraction and intensive examination of mundane examples.

A childlike turn of mind facilitates the dialog.   This non-combative innocence is an important ingredient for good dialog as well as for modeling in general.

The participants in the dialog usually include the experts or specialists in the field being explored as well as modeling specialists. Both roles are required.

Frequently, as the dialog continues, we see specialists interchanging roles. This is an indication that things are going well: The modelers are gaining enough understanding to really talk with the experts!

Note the term "dialog" (as opposed to "interview"). The sense of equality of participation is a critical success factor.

If the dialog idea is strange to you, try to sit in on such a session. You will soon get the flavor of the proceedings—at this point, just join in.

When your mind goes completely blank, here are some good questions to ask. They have been labeled with key words that may help you to formulate other questions.

Fishing. "Tell us about the widget." (The answer will contain attributes of widgets plus, possibly, some other objects and their attributes.)

Multiplicity. "How many widgets are there?"

Relatedness. "How does the widget relate to the gizmo?" (Here "relate" is being used non-technically.)

Without. "Would the gizmo still be valid (real, still work, and so forth) if we took away the widget?" "Can you ever have a Form B without a request form?" This line of questioning often helps to isolate objects and identify referential attributes.

Walking between objects. "What else is related to/connected to the gizmo?"

Other ways to get here. "Is there any way that you can get a Form B, without first having a Form A?"

Viewpoints. "How does the foreman (president, clerk, . . .) use/think about Form B?"

Other dialog pointers:

1. Change the name of an object or attribute from its specialist term to a functional term, at least for purposes of discussion. Multiword, hyphenated names are okay for working sessions (eventually you will want to tidy them up, but only after you're sure what they mean).
2. Keep feeding back to the application specialist: "Ok, let's see if I got this right . . ."
3. Keep summarizing: "We have a gizmo and these are its attributes. It is connected to . . ."
4. Work bottom up, regardless of what is in style this year.

8.3 TECHNICAL NOTES

Good old-fashioned technical writing is often what is needed to turn information into understanding. We encourage our analysts to write technical notes—two- or three-page <u>single</u> <u>topic</u> memos. This is especially useful early in the analysis phase, when you haven't yet sorted out enough of the problem to make good progress on the information model itself.

There can be an unexpected benefit later: The technical note file might contain much of the text that is needed for object descriptions.

Consider writing a technical note after any interview, phone conference, site visit, or similar activity.

A normal analysis project (if there is such a thing) will generate 20 to 200 technical notes. It is a good idea to publish a list of these technical notes so that all participants can be kept up to date.

8.4 REVIEWS

An Information Model should be subjected to intensive critical review to ensure that it represents an accurate reflection of the world problem. The review can be formal or informal; to be effective, it is necessary that people other than those who constructed the model be involved.

A useful state of mind for the review process comes from a "medical consultation" image: Here we have a patient. We have called in a number of specialists to examine the patient to determine what, if anything, is wrong with him.

Most Important: The focus of the review should always be on the *work* (the model), never on the workers who produced it. Flaws in the model should be seen primarily as interesting symptoms, not as evidence of less than adequate performance on the part of the model builders. (Flaws are most commonly due to communication failures, anyway.)

When reviewing a model, make sure that you read each sentence slowly and literally. You may find "boo-boos" like:

"An access point is a description of..." (No, it's a location.)

". . . date on which payment was received from the customer who is responsible for the account." (No, payment can be received from anybody.)

It is *normal* to go through two or three rounds of review on a substantial model.

8.5 OTHER SUGGESTIONS

1. If there is an existing system that you are working to upgrade, arrange for a one-day visit, but not until you have done a little background preparation (or else you won't know what you are seeing).   It is difficult to predict what you will learn on such a site visit, but it always seems to be valuable.

2. Keep a loose-ends list containing questions that you are still researching, known model flaws, documents to run down, and the like.   This helps to keep one from getting overwhelmed with chores, as well as preventing premature iterations of the model.

3. Many process control systems are associated with some kind of control room or control center where the operators—meaning the ultimate users of the system—do their work.   It may be useful to spend a number of days in the control room, learning as much as possible of the operator's job.   If there is an operator's training course, it might be a good idea to take it.

4. If the action in the control room is too fast to follow (or if the control room doesn't exist yet), make a mock-up.   We once mocked up a chemical plant by taping schematic drawings to a table top and using slips of colored paper to represent the states of valves ("red you're closed, green you're open").   Watching experienced operators at work on such a "plant" can rapidly clear up a lot of questions.   This is also an excellent way to investigate operator's heuristics.

Chapter 9

The Role of the Information Model in System Development

Information modeling can be useful in many kinds of situations where there is something systematic going on that needs to be elucidated. For example, consider formalization of expert knowledge for wider use within a company. Perhaps the company—a supplier of office telephone systems—has a crackerjack configuration engineer: someone who has built up a great deal of know-how and insight in figuring out whether or not a proposed set of telephones, cards, cables, and software options can be put together to compose an operational telephone system with the desired features. Information modeling would be useful here for extracting, from the engineer, the special way of thinking about configuration that he has developed. If there is anything systematic about his approach—and we presume there is—we will be able to capture the conceptual units of his mental model and the relationships he relies on to evaluate configuration alternatives.

A similar situation frequently arises in both the business data processing world and in industrial and manufacturing applications: Some kind of process has been developed over time. The process may be entirely paper-based or it may involve some number of computer systems. In either case, it turns out that nowhere in the organization is there someone who understands it all. Instead, the company's understanding is distributed over a number of experts, each of whom has special knowledge, conventions, and practices. Great difficulties arise when it is time to modify the process: You can't tell what you can change without bringing down the whole operation. Information modeling is especially useful in such a situation since it can be used to integrate the diverse views of all the experts, and so bring out in the open the information on which the process is based.

Note that in both of the above examples there was lurking the idea of a system: a unit that can supply predictable and appropriate responses to given stimuli or input. There was no necessary implication that a computer was to be involved or that software was to be built.

Nonetheless, information models are usually thought of in the context of software development for automated systems. In these special cases, can the information model do more than just serve as a fundamental thinking tool for problem understanding?

This chapter is concerned with answering that question. In subsequent sections we outline an overall software development process which makes repeated use of the information model.

9.1 SOFTWARE DEVELOPMENT PROCESSES

First of all, the reader should be warned that, in the authors' opinions, there is no single right software development process suitable for all situations. Good choices of software development processes are influenced by numerous factors, including:

— developer familiarity with the application area
— existence of software which might be incorporated into the system to be constructed
— expertise of developers: How much skill do they have and in what areas?
— responsibility for software construction: Your company needs a computer system to solve a particular problem. Will your company buy it off the shelf, have someone build it to order, or build it in-house?

With the caveat ("no single right way"), we present here the outline of a software development process that we have found to be effective and adaptable over a reasonable range of situations. This process breaks out into four phases:

1. Analysis of the Problem
2. External Specification
3. System Design
4. Implementation and Integration

The phases are described below in varying degrees of detail.

9.2 THE ANALYSIS PHASE: AN OBJECT-ORIENTED APPROACH

9.2.1 Objects and the Information Model

The first thing to do is to build the information model to define the conceptual units you will be working with. In doing this it is important to stay focused on the real world—the problem—and not the solution to that problem, which will be supplied with the automated computer system.

It is assumed that you know the approximate "center" of the problem domain, and you will start there to identify objects. If you can't identify the center, start anywhere and just keep working. Continue until you have objects that are at least one layer outside the scope of the system to be built. Since you won't know the formal scope of the system for a while yet, be generous: Extra objects lead only to extra understanding, which cannot be a bad thing.

9.2.2 States of Objects and State Models

Life Cycles.   Once the information model has been built, one notes that instances of some objects can be regarded as undergoing a kind of "life cycle." For example, consider an Account object. Initially, the Account may be regarded as nonexistent. Then a customer appears and makes a deposit, thus bringing the account into existence. In this state, the customer may make further deposits or withdrawals until the balance of the account is less than or equal to zero. The account must now be regarded as being in a different state: overdrawn. Now only deposits can be accepted; withdrawals cannot. A deposit that leaves the balance positive will cause the account to change its state again. Eventually, the customer will close the account causing the account to reach yet another state (closed); in other words, the Account has come to the end of its life cycle and ceases to exist.

State Transition Diagrams.   The life cycle concept can be formalized with the aid of a state model. Such a model can be shown in a graphical representation known as a state transition diagram, as shown in Figure 9.1. In this diagram, each rectangular box denotes a *state*. A state represents a stage in the life cycle for instances of the object concerned. Note that each account can be in a different state at any given time. The diagram holds for each instance of the Account object separately since, by definition of any object, all instances must have the same behavior. Behavior over time is really what is being formalized by the state model.

The arrows shown on the state transition diagram are *transitions* which take place when an *event* occurs. The event is written next to the transition to show what causes the transition. Note that several transitions may leave a given state as long as the events that cause the transition in each case are different. It is also possible for a transition to be made from one state to the same state.

The final component of the diagram is the *action*. Actions are associated

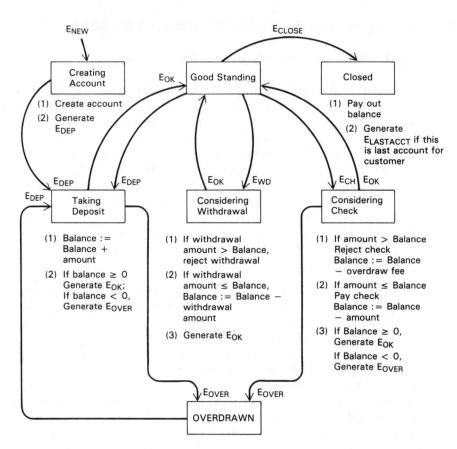

Figure 9.1 State Transition Diagram for Account

with states, so that on entry to a state all the associated actions are caused to take place.

One can "execute" a state transition diagram as follows: Starting from any given state, an event occurs that causes a transition to some other (possibly the same) state. On entry to the state, the associated actions are carried out. The instance is now in a new state, and nothing happens to this particular instance until another event occurs.

A final note: For any object that has a life cycle, include a status attribute in the information model (Account.Status, for example). The domain of this attribute is simply a list of the states appearing in the corresponding state model.

Coordination of States. Picking up the Account example, again, let us consider the Customer object. Account and Customer must be coordinated in some way; let us suppose that the information model expresses at least some of this by a relationship Customer HOLDS Accounts (1:M). The same coordination can be shown at the instance level through state models for the Account and Customer objects. This is done through events. In this case, the Account state model generates events that affect the Customer state model.

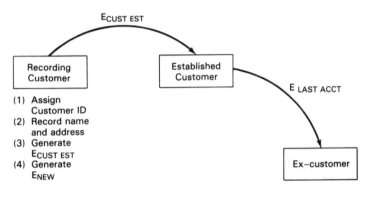

Figure 9.2   State Transition Diagram for the Customer Object

9.2.3 Actions and Data Flow Diagrams

Upon inspecting the actions on a state model, it soon becomes apparent that, while cryptic, they have a "process" or "data transformation" nature. What can be done to illuminate this aspect of the problem?

The data flow diagram [De Marco 1977] is a graphic tool for modeling transformations and manipulations of data. We use data flow diagrams to expose the detail of the actions from the state models. For an example, see Figure 9.3, which shows the actions associated with the Account object.

The figure illustrates the three components of a data flow diagram:

— data flows, which are represented by labeled arrows;
— processes, represented by circles; and
— stores, shown as pairs of parallel lines.

The stores are derived directly from the objects of the information model and are

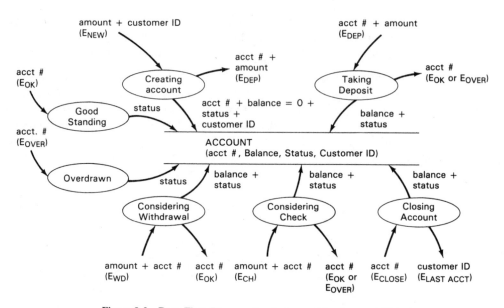

Figure 9.3 Data Flow Diagram for Actions of the Account Object

named to correspond. You can think of the stores as tables that have been filled out with data to represent the existing instances.

The data flows are the active units of data—packets of data containing the named attributes. When a data flow "arrives," it is acted on by a process, which may also draw data from stores as required to do its job. Note that because each piece of data is an attribute, its meaning is already defined in the information model. For this reason it is not necessary to provide a separate "data dictionary," as would be the case if the data flow diagrams were not based on the information model, as they are here.

To specify exactly what a process must do, one provides a detailed description for each process. Process descriptions can be rendered through a variety of notations and languages, including narrative natural-language text, mathematics, a pseudocode based on relational query languages, and decision trees. All that matters is that the language or formalism chosen should be appropriate for the process to be described: A mathematical description of an information query would be a poor choice, as would a narrative description of the calculation of a Bessel function or a tax payment. In some cases, the process may be so trivial or obvious as to warrant no specification at all.

9.2.4 Integrating the Analysis Models

The analysis models state the conceptual units of the problem (the objects), the life cycle that the instances of each conceptual unit go through, and the processing required to draw each unit through its life cycle. These aspects of the problem

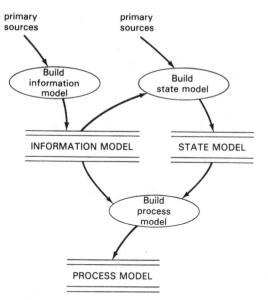

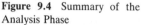

Figure 9.4 Summary of the Analysis Phase

domain are expressed in the information model, the state model, and the data flow diagram respectively. The models are integrated, with the information model providing the foundations for the other two as follows:

— State transition diagrams are built for the objects that exhibit a life cycle or operational cycle.
— State transitions cause actions to take place. These actions are represented as processes on a data flow diagram.
— Each object on the information model becomes a store on the data flow diagram.
— Processes accept and produce only the data which is defined in the information model.
— Processes may create events which appear on the state transition diagram.

It is these relationships between the information, state, and process models which lead to the structure of the Analysis Phase shown in Figure 9.4.

9.3 THE EXTERNAL SPECIFICATION PHASE

9.3.1 What is an External Specification?

The analysis documents, taken together, provide an abstract model of a system: an information-based entity that behaves in a systematic, defined, and predictable manner to inputs or stimuli. They do not, however, say how computers are involved. Putting it in terms of processes, the analysis documents do not say which processes are to be carried out by computers and which are to be carried out by people. The purpose of the external specification phase is to make decisions about what the computer should do and what it should not do.

To illustrate, consider a banking problem. The analysis shows that there are such things as checks, and that a check may be presented at the bank to be cashed. When this occurs, the bank must verify that (1) there is enough money in the account to honor the check, and (2) that the signature on the check is that of the customer on whose account the check was written. What the analysis documents *do not* say is who will do which elements of the preceding jobs. The task of the external specification is to state which of many alternatives has been chosen. For example, in the banking problem, the external specification would state which of the following alternative schemes had been selected:

— The teller might type in the amount of the check and the account number and let a computer say "Balance OK" or "Not OK."

— The teller might type in the account number, and have the computer provide the current account balance. The teller would then compare the balance with the amount of the check, and make the determination of "Balance OK" or "Not OK."

— The teller might look up the signature on a signature card, using the account number as the index. The teller would compare the signature on the check with that on the signature card.

— The teller might type in the account number and have the computer present an image of the signature card. The teller would compare the signatures.

— The teller might slide the check into a high-resolution image reader. The computer would process the check image, determining the account number and the amount of the check. It would also isolate the signature, and compare the signature against a pre-stored image. Based on all of this information, the computer would make an "OK to cash/Not OK" decision.

Deciding between such alternatives is a difficult job, since it involves identifying possible implementations, determining the cost of each possibility, and determining the amount of money that would be saved by each choice. There are frequently additional dimensions that are important to the decisions: time to implement, confidence in the time and cost estimates, reliability of the proposed solution, and the like.

There is today no well-developed systematic way to make tradeoffs involving all the various relevant dimensions. Given this, the most rational strategy we know is to isolate the problem: Make certain that when you are making such decisions, you are making *only* those decisions. It is for this reason (among others) that we lead into the external specification phase by the analysis phase.

9.3.2 Stating the Specification by Stating the Boundary

One strategy that may be used to state the external specification is to focus on the automation boundary—the imaginary line between the portion of the abstract system to be held in computers and the portion to be left outside. An external specification based on the concept of boundary provides basically a "black box" description of the system to be built.

Such an external specification can be based on the concept of *external events*: those events of the state models which cross the automation boundary. The specification document can be cast in several forms, including the external event list and the narrative requirements document as described below.

9.3.2.1 External event list.   An *external event list* is simply a concise list of the events which occur just outside the automation boundary and require action to take place inside the automated portion of the system. Each event should be keyed to the analysis model (which provides the meaning and definition of action required) and listed together with the data that is required to accompany it.

This form of specification is extremely economical, but is unlikely to be acceptable if the external specification must form the basis of a contract for software development. In our view, this is not due to any technical unworkability of the method, but instead to a practical issue: It is not common practice for such a document to serve as a contract.

9.3.2.2 Narrative requirements documents.   A narrative requirements document (sometimes called "functional requirements" or "functional specification") uses natural language to state what the automated system must do. Such a document can be produced in a concise and organized manner by translating an external event list into text.

It has become fashionable, lately, to deride forms of specification based on narrative text. The weaknesses commonly ascribed to the narrative form are:

— redundancy
— lack of precision: different readers interpret the same statement differently
— incompleteness (or difficulty in evaluating for completeness)
— inability to evaluate for internal consistency
— inability to reveal implications of the stated requirements
— length and organization: the documents are generally too long to read and assimilate

These very serious weaknesses are not due, in our opinion, to the use of natural language. Instead, they arise from the fact that most narrative requirements documents are not based on a systematic view of the problem: Such a document is generally asked to bear the burden of the analysis itself.

The situation is greatly improved when the requirements document is backed up by the abstract system (analysis) models. The information model defines the vocabulary in a careful and systematic way; the state models clearly reveal intrinsic constraints of the problem as well as the implications of making any particular event an external one; the information, state, and data flow models are cast purposefully to reduce redundancy to a minimum, and the information model provides an extremely powerful basis for evaluation of completeness.

9.3.3 Stating the Specification by Stating What's Inside

Alternatively, the external specification can be developed by focusing on the portions of the abstract system (analysis) model that will be placed inside the computers. This orientation is similar to such traditional formulations of the system specification problem as:

— What is the *scope* of the automated system?
— What *operations* will the automated system carry out?

The external specification documents can therefore be cast directly on the analysis models: One can record the "what's inside" decisions by going through the analysis documents and marking each element (object, attribute, relationship, event, transition, state, and process) that is to be placed inside the computer.

There are two disadvantages of the "what's inside" orientation. The less serious disadvantage is that, in a sense, too much information is supplied by such a specification. While all of the implications of a "what's inside" decision are clearly visible, the detail of the specification provides many opportunities for distraction in the review process. In effect, the analysis model is being reviewed at the same time as the external specification.

The more serious disadvantage is that such a specification is likely to be misinterpreted and read as a statement of system design. This is very definitely not appropriate: An external specification is only a statement of what the system is to do, not a statement of how the system is to accomplish its assignments. Most external specifications are open to several alternative system designs (developed during the design phase, described below). However, it appears that only the most experienced system designers and architects are able to see such design alternatives, and so avoid misinterpreting the specification.

9.3.4 Other Dimensions of External Specification

The external specification, as developed so far, describes only the information content of the transactions that cross the system boundary. The format of those transactions needs to be stated in order to provide a complete "black box" specification of the automated system.   This is done by producing descriptions of as many of the following as are relevant to the situation at hand:

— screen layouts
— report formats
— detailed descriptions of any interfaces with other automated systems
— operator procedures

Taken together, these requirements state *how* the system will appear to an external user.

In addition, it is also often necessary to state at this time any performance requirements, reliability requirements, and the like.

9.3.5 Integrating the External Specification Phase

In the external specification phase, only two pieces of information are being added. First, there is a statement of the system boundary, and second, there is a statement of how the system appears to those who interact with it.   This new information is strongly supported by the analysis models, and particularly the information model. The information crossing the boundary is defined in terms of attributes, and the narrative requirements use vocabulary that is defined by the object and relationship descriptions.   The statement of the external interface is also stated in terms of attributes.   The steps in the external specification phase are shown in Figure 9.5.

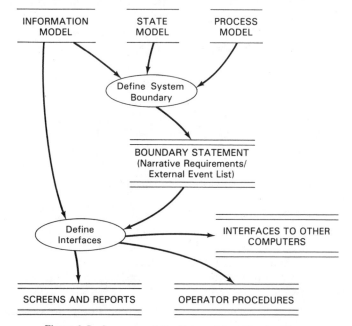

Figure 9.5   Summary of the External Specification Phase

9.4 THE SYSTEM DESIGN PHASE

At this point in the development life cycle, there is a clear definition of what information is to be retained by the automated system, and the operations required to act on it.   A complete specification of the system has been constructed, and it must now be handed over to systems developers.

The fundamental questions that must be addressed in this phase of the software development involve issues that must be decided for the system as a whole, rather than for an individual program or a single data structure.   These are the cosmic decisions which, if made well, will outlive all of the programming.   They include:

— What will be the systemwide rules for organization of shared data?

— What systemwide rules will control access to that data (to ensure consistency)?

— Are there to be any rules that each program must obey (such as standard input/standard output as in UNIX)?

— What data needs to be in the system?

— What will be the rationale for division of the required processing into programs?

— What programs are to be built?

In the general case, many of these questions must be addressed at least partially in parallel with one another.   The following represents one breakdown of the design work; we assume that these steps are done in parallel to the extent required.

9.4.1 Software Architecture Design

This step declares the system-wide rules for:

— organization and access to shared data

— triggering programs (how a program is to be told when to run)

— any conventions required on the programs themselves.   These conventions have to do with interfaces between programs, and are derived from the data organization, data access, and program triggering rules.

There may be almost no work required in software architecture.   You might, for example, determine that such-and-such a commercially-available database system is to be used to organize and control access to the shared data, that every program can be invoked by a user at a terminal at any time, and that the only conventions required on the programs to prevent interference are those imposed by the database software itself.

On the other hand, if you have a real-time process control system or similar multiple-program problem, a great deal of work may be required to figure out the software architecture rules and how they are to be enforced.

9.4.2 Design of System Information Content

Here one decides what information needs to be available in the automated system. This can be determined fairly easily by examining the data flow diagrams of the analysis to determine what data is required by the processes. The results of this examination are expressed in a Reduced Information Model.

The reduced information model is constructed by examining each attribute to find out if it is required by any operation in the automated system. If no operation uses the attribute, it may be discarded. If all the attributes of an object are discarded, the object itself is also discarded.

Note that when a referential attribute is removed, the implication is that no operation traverses the relationship and that the automated system is unaware that such a relationship exists in the real world. The relationship has been discarded.

The reduced information model can be conveniently rendered as an information structure diagram that shows only the retained objects, attributes, and relationships. Since all of these elements were described in detail in the Information Model, there is no need to duplicate the descriptions.

9.4.3 Data Structure Design

Now that the information that must be carried by a system has been identified, the next step is to translate the conceptual view of the data into the data structures used for implementation. This structure can vary from uniform structures supported by a database management system accessed by many programs to data structures held within a single program.

Of major importance in many applications is the speed of access to the data. To decide on an appropriate structure, it is helpful to examine the operations required by the systems to be built in order to determine:

— whether the relationships are traversed in one direction or both by operations
— the frequency of access, to the objects and relationships, by the operations
— when the operations occur (all at once in a nightly run, or distributed evenly throughout the day in online transactions)

Note that tradeoffs must be made during the data structure design step: The reduced information model gives one possible way to structure the data. This structure has minimal data redundancy and provides unbiased ease of access to all data elements (that is, the structure lets you trace data across all relationships with an approximately equal number of searches). Any distortion of this structure will introduce data redundancy and will enhance the ease of access across certain relationships, while simultaneously making other access paths more difficult. As a general rule, then, we seek to produce data structures that mirror the reduced information model to the greatest extent possible while still satisfying performance requirements. In this way, we minimize the access paths which are being made inefficient: a desirable goal in situations where you believe that new requirements may come along which will necessitate unanticipated access patterns.

9.4.4 Partitioning into Programs

To have a coherent system, one needs to develop a rationale for dividing the required processing into programs. There are numerous possibilities. For example, one might decide to write one object-oriented program for each state model shown in the analysis. This produces an implementation where the code is highly application-dependent: The code tends to be minimally reuseable, but very clear and easy to read.

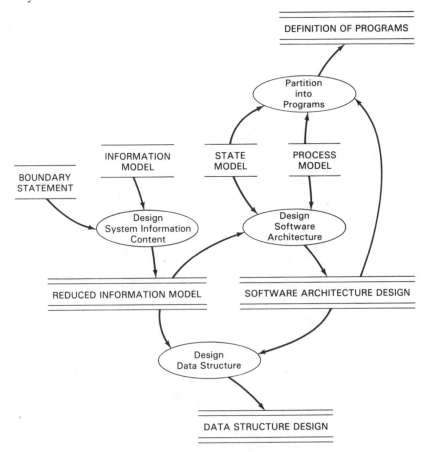

Figure 9.6   Summary of the System Design Phase

Another partitioning rationale would be to develop a master state model processor, and encode the state models themselves in data. The action routines would be cast as a set of subroutines, invoked as required by the events as they are accepted and decoded. This strategy will lead to somewhat less code and many fewer headaches, since the code is forced to be well structured in order to interface with the state model processor.

A third rationale, sometimes used for only part of the system, is to group computationally alike operations together. This leads to a few programs, temporally organized. Many process control systems are constructed on this rationale: one program to collect the raw data, one program to convert the raw data to engineering units and file it in the shared data structures, a further program to develop data values that are derived from the engineering unit data, a checking program to verify values in correct range, and a program to calculate feedback signals that are required to be returned to the plant.

Whatever the rationale, it should be clearly stated. Once this has been done, the programs to be built should be listed together with their input and output data, cast as objects and attributes.

9.4.5 Summary of the System Design Phase

Whereas in previous phases the information model was valuable for the application knowledge it conveyed, in the System Design Phase it plays a different role: that of conveying the intrinsic structure of the information that the system must process. This use of the information model is shown in Figure 9.6, which summarizes the System Design Phase of the software development process.

9.5 THE IMPLEMENTATION PHASE

The implementation phase is concerned with getting the data and programs prepared and tested.

9.5.1 Data Collection

This aspect of implementation is driven primarily from the reduced information model.

The reduced information model should be inspected to see if there is any appreciable amount of static data (data that isn't modified during operation) that is required in the automated system. If so, it may pay to take a systematic approach toward obtaining and verifying that data. The steps in such a systematic approach include:

1. *Identification of Sources.* Survey the potential sources of the data, make some determination about the reliability of competing sources, and select the sources to be used.

2. *Develop Entry Procedures.* Decide how the data must be prepared for entry. Comprehensive manual procedures may need to be prescribed, particularly when data must be obtained from paper sources (including engineering prints, etc.). It is frequently necessary to build some programs to assist the entry procedures, particularly when the data is coming from computer-readable sources.

3. *Prepare Data Structures.* Encode the data structures previously designed into the computer. The details of this task depend on the software being used to handle systemwide data: If a commercially-available database system is employed, this step requires the preparation and processing of the schema.

4. *Enter Data.* Prepare the data, enter it into the formats prescribed by the entry procedures, and process it into the permanent shared data structures.

5. *Verification.* The data should be inspected for correctness. This may be as simple as printing and examining reports and possibly comparing the reports against alternative data sources. Depending on the nature of the relationships maintained in the automated system, it may be possible to prescribe some simple verification programs that check the data to see that the relationships are being properly preserved.

9.5.2 Program Design

In this step the programs are parceled out to implementation specialists for design. Each implementor needs to be provided with the program's interface description (developed in the *Partitioning into Programs* step) as well as the data structure design previously developed and the applicable architectural rules.

The primary tool applicable to design of the internal structure of a program is the structure chart [Yourdon and Constantine, 1978; Page-Jones, 1980].

9.5.3 Code and Test

This step consists of the construction of the programs themselves in accordance with the program design. Each module should be coded and tested separately, and then progressively integrated, each module with its callers or subordinates, to produce the program. This step should be interpreted literally to mean that coding is complete only when the program is also tested as a unit.

9.5.4 Integration and Acceptance

Integration consists of putting the various programs and data together to produce a system. The integration step starts with programs that have been tested, each by itself, and with data that has been verified, as previously discussed. Integration is the step that verifies that these separate units, each as correct as can be made on its own, will in fact fit together to make the required system. In other words, integration is the test of the *system* design.

The experienced system designer, therefore, pays a lot of attention to what will happen during integration. He or she will prescribe a system design that can be integrated piece by piece, and that contains test points and features at the architectural level to allow careful monitoring and confirmation of the systemwide behavior as integration progresses. In addition, the system designer will anticipate that some programs will escape the net of careful review and come to integration in violation of the rules that were laid down in the software architecture. There-

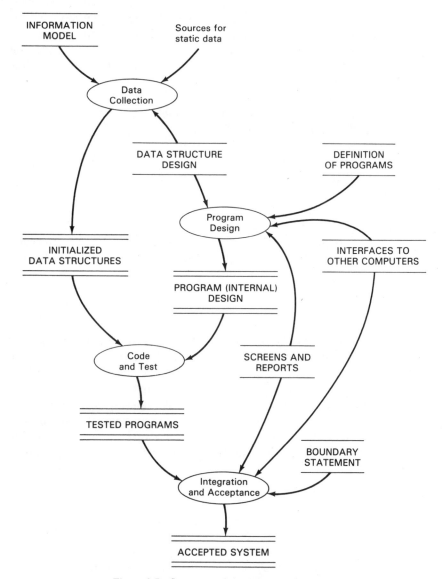

Figure 9.7   Summary of the Implementation Phase

fore, protective measures may be taken in the system design itself as a way of catching these lawbreakers, lest a protracted integration phase reflect poorly on the design.

Finally, *acceptance* is the check that the collection of programs, that was integrated in the previous step, truly meets the external specification; that is, the system does what it was supposed to do. The "buyer" of the system must be convinced that the system does what was originally requested.

Note that both integration and acceptance require good planning well in advance of their execution. In addition, both should be largely a matter of verifying that our work has been correct. Since each step in the software development process has been derived carefully and systematically from the previous steps, and each has been intensively reviewed, integration and acceptance should *not* be a euphemism for rework.

9.5.5 The Role of the Information Model in the Implementation Phase

The Implementation Phase consists of the actual construction of the system and a final check that the constructed system, indeed, does the job for which it was intended.

With the exception of the data collection step, the information model enters into the final phase of the software development process only indirectly: through materials produced in earlier phases that were derived in part from the information model. A summary of the Implementation Phase is shown in Figure 9.7.

9.6 SUMMARY

We have laid out an example of a software development process that makes repeated use of the information model. The development process has been divided roughly into four phases: analysis, external specification, system design, and implementation. In each step, the information model has played a significant role, most particularly in the early stages. In the later stages, the information model is applied chiefly in data structure or database design—the traditional use of such a model. However, because the operations were derived from the life cycles of the objects, the information model has also had a strong, if less direct, impact on the code.

Appendix   A

Information Model
for Management
of Magnetic Tapes

This information model is concerned with the management of magnetic tapes and related equipment in a computer center.   A graphical representation of the model is given together with the various object and attribute descriptions that comprise the textual representation of the model.   The purpose of this appendix is to convey an understanding of the amount of work that might be required in developing an information model of a real-world problem.

Part I: Graphical Representation of the Model

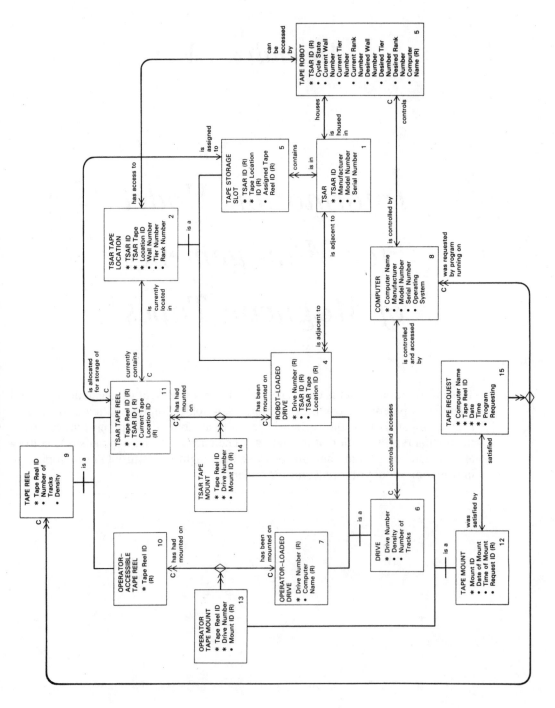

Part II: Objects and Attributes

1. TSAR

TSAR (TSAR ID, Manufacturer, Model Number, Serial Number)

Identifiers:

TSAR ID

Manufacturer + Model Number + Serial Number

Description: A tape store and retrieval unit (TSAR) is a housing about 10 feet long, 7 feet high, and 8 feet wide. Inside the TSAR are several thousand storage slots in which reels of magnetic tape can be placed. The TSAR is equipped with a robot which can be directed to travel about within the TSAR and to move magnetic tapes from one slot to another.

Arranged adjacent to the TSAR are several magnetic tape drives. These tape drives have been positioned in such a way that the robot can reach and manipulate them in order to mount and dismount tapes.

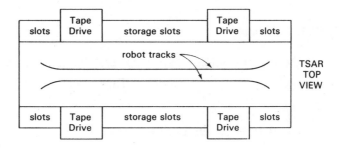

The slots used for storage of tape are located along the long (10 foot) walls of the TSAR housing.

1.1 TSAR.TSAR ID

Each TSAR has been assigned an identifier which is used by the operations and maintenance staff to distinguish between the TSARs in service at the computer center. The identifier is a single alphabetic character, painted conspicuously on the TSAR housing itself.

The TSAR identifiers are assigned by the Chief of Operations.

Domain: See above

1.2 TSAR.Manufacturer

This attribute records the name of the manufacturer of the TSAR.

Domain: manufacturer names

1.3 TSAR.Model Number

At the moment, there are several kinds of TSARs in service, which differ in minor ways. Some models have storage slots along both of the long walls of the housing; other models have only one long wall so equipped. In addition, the storage slots on some models are closer together, providing a closer packing and, therefore, a larger number of tapes can be placed in the same sized housing. Details on these and other minor differences between models of TSARs can be found in the manufacturer's technical and maintenance manuals.

The Model Number attribute records the manufacturer-stated model number for the TSAR.

Domain: model numbers (as stated by the manufacturers)

1.4 TSAR.Serial Number

Every TSAR housing is given a serial number at the time of manufacture. This attribute records that serial number, as bestowed by the manufacturer of the TSAR.

Domain: serial numbers, as given by the manufacturers

2. TSAR TAPE LOCATION

> TSAR Tape Location (TSAR ID, Wall Number, Tier Number, Rank Number, Tape Location ID)

Identifiers:

> TSAR ID + Tape Location ID
>
> TSAR ID + Wall Number + Tier Number + Rank Number

Description: Associated with each TSAR are a number of defined tape locations which can be reached by the tape robot. These locations fall into two types: (1) the tape storage slots (see object description for Tape Storage Slot) and (2) the magnetic tape drives accessible by the robot. The TSAR Tape Location object provides the formalization of both types of tape location within the TSARs.

Within a given TSAR, the tape locations are arranged along one or both of the long walls. Every tape location on a given wall is known by its "tier number," which is proportional to the vertical distance from the floor of the TSAR housing, and a "rank number," which is proportional to the horizontal distance from the left end of the wall as the robot faces it. The basic scheme for tape locations is shown in the following sketch.

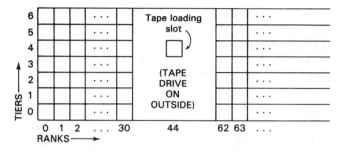

Note that each of the magnetic tape drives has been assigned a tier number and a rank number, corresponding to the correct horizontal and vertical position for directing the robot.

TSARs, walls, tiers, and ranks form a natural identification scheme for TSAR tape locations.   Note, however, that not all combinations of tier number and rank number correspond to a place where the robot can put a tape, since there are no tape storage slots in the area where the tape drives abut the TSAR housing.

2.1 TSAR Tape Location.TSAR ID

Each tape location accessible by a tape robot is identified by the TSAR within which it lies plus a wall number, tier number, and rank number within the TSAR. This attribute provides the TSAR component of the identifier of the tape location.
Domain: Same as TSAR.TSAR ID

2.2 TSAR Tape Location.Wall Number

Each wall of the TSAR housing has been assigned a number (0 or 1) to identify it.   This attribute tells on which wall the tape location has been placed.
Domain: wall numbers

2.3 TSAR Tape Location.Tier Number

The tape locations within the TSAR are arranged in horizontal rows, or tiers. Each tier of tape slots is assigned a tier number, which is proportional to the distance of the tier from the floor of the housing.   Tiers are numbered from 0 at the bottom to 6 at the top of the wall.
Domain: tier numbers

2.4 TSAR Tape Location.Rank Number

Each tape location is assigned a rank number, which is proportional to the distance of the tape location from one end of the wall.   Rank numbers start at zero at the left end of the wall (as seen by the robot), and continue to a maximum value at the right end.

Domain: rank numbers

2.5 TSAR Tape Location.Tape Location ID

This attribute provides an arbitrary identifier, created for the purposes of this model, for a tape location within a TSAR. The attribute was created to provide a concise way of modeling the subtype/supertype relationship that prevails between the TSAR Tape Location object and the Tape Storage Slots/Robot-Loaded Drive objects.

The domain of this attribute is arbitrary. Should such an identifier be required in implementation of an automated system, the domain could be defined as integers. Alternatively, a naming scheme based on the TSAR ID, wall number, tier number, and rank number could be devised.

Domain: See above

3. TAPE STORAGE SLOT

Tape Storage Slot (TSAR ID, TSAR Tape Location ID,

Assigned Tape Reel ID)

Identifiers:

TSAR ID + TSAR Tape Location ID

Description: A Tape Storage Slot is a TSAR Tape Location that is used for storage of magnetic tapes within the TSAR. The tape locations corresponding to the robot-loaded magnetic tape drives are not considered to be tape storage slots.

3.1 Tape Storage Slot.TSAR ID

This attribute tells which TSAR contains the tape storage slot, and so formalizes the relationship Tape Storage Slot IS IN TSAR.

Domain: Same as TSAR.TSAR ID

3.2 Tape Storage Slot.TSAR Tape Location ID

Each tape storage slot is regarded as being a tape location. This attribute provides the identifier of the tape location that corresponds to this tape storage slot, and so formalizes the relationship Tape Storage Slot IS A (SUBTYPE OF) TSAR Tape Location.

Domain: Same as TSAR Tape Location.Tape Location ID

3.3 Tape Storage Slot.Assigned Tape Reel ID

Each tape reel selected for storage within a TSAR is assigned to a tape storage slot. This attribute tells which reel, if any, is assigned to this tape storage slot, and so formalizes the relationship TSAR Tape Reel IS ASSIGNED TO Tape Storage Slot.

Domain: This domain is composed of the union of { no tape assigned } and the domain of TSAR Tape Reel.Tape Reel ID.

4. ROBOT-LOADED DRIVE

Robot-Loaded Drive (Drive Number, TSAR ID, TSAR Tape
Location ID)

Identifiers:

Drive Number

TSAR ID + Tape Location ID

Description: A Robot-Loaded Drive is a magnetic tape drive that has been specially constructed to allow loading of tapes on it by a tape robot. In every other regard, a Robot-Loaded Drive is an entirely standard tape drive.

4.1 Robot-Loaded Drive.Drive Number

Every magnetic tape drive in the facility is assigned a unique drive number by the operations staff. This attribute provides the drive number for a robot-loaded tape drive.

See also the description of Drive.Drive Number.

This attribute is used to establish the relationship Robot-Loaded Drive IS A (SUBTYPE OF) Drive.

Domain: Same as Drive.Drive Number

4.2 Robot-Loaded Drive.TSAR ID

Each robot-loaded drive is placed adjacent to a TSAR housing in such a way that the tape loading station of the drive lines up with a special loading slot on the TSAR housing. This attribute formalizes the relationship Robot-Loaded Drive IS ADJACENT TO TSAR.

Domain: Same as TSAR.TSAR ID

4.3 Robot-Loaded Drive.TSAR Tape Location ID

Each robot-loaded drive can be viewed as a tape location within a TSAR, in that it provides a place to which the robot can deliver tapes. This situation is reflected in the model by the relationship Robot-Loaded Drive IS A (SUBTYPE OF) TSAR Tape Location.

This attribute, together with Robot-Loaded Drive.TSAR ID, formalizes the relationship Robot-Loaded Drive IS A TSAR Tape Location.

Domain: Same as TSAR Tape Location.Tape Location ID

5. TAPE ROBOT

> Tape Robot (TSAR ID, Cycle State, Current
> Wall Number, Desired Wall Number,
> Current Tier Number, Desired
> Tier Number, Current Rank Number,
> Desired Rank Number,
> Computer Name)

Identifiers:

TSAR ID

Description: A tape robot is a mechanical device that is capable of fetching a tape from a tape location in a TSAR, travelling to another point in the TSAR, and depositing the tape in a new tape location. The tape robot runs on tracks fixed to the floor of the TSAR housing.

The tape robot is a computer-controllable device.

5.1 Tape Robot.TSAR ID

Each tape robot is housed in exactly one TSAR. This attribute tells the name of the TSAR in which the robot is housed, and so formalizes the relationship Tape Robot IS HOUSED IN TSAR.

Domain: Same as TSAR.TSAR ID

5.2 Tape Robot.Cycle State

The motions that the tape robot goes through are described as states in an operational cycle. Under normal circumstances, the robot progresses serially through states 1 to 6, as follows:

1. Idle. The robot is motionless and ready to accept a new "tape move" command.

2. Accepting Command. The robot is accepting a "tape move" command. Each tape move command specifies a source wall, source tier, and source rank, as well as a target wall, target tier, and target rank. The meaning of the command is to move a tape from the source to the target location.

3. Seeking Source. The robot is moving to the source tape location.

4. At Source. The robot is positioned in front of the source tape location and is picking up the tape.

5. Seeking Target. The robot is moving to the target tape location.

6. At Target. The robot is positioned in front of the target tape location and is depositing the tape. Following this state, the robot will return to the Idle state.

There are also several error states:

7. No Tape at Source. If the robot enters this state, the computer must issue a "robot reset" command to return the robot to the Idle state.

8. Dropped Tape. This state occurs if the robot ever picks up the source tape, but loses it before depositing it at the target tape location. If the robot enters this state, the operations staff must enter the TSAR housing and pick up the dropped tape; after which the computer must issue a "robot reset" command to return the robot to the Idle state.

9. Reset with Tape in Hand. This state occurs if a "robot reset" command is given when the robot is carrying a tape.

Domain: [idle | accepting command | seeking source | at source | seeking target | at target | no tape at source | dropped tape | reset with tape in hand]

5.3 Tape Robot.Current Wall Number

The wall currently being accessed by the tape robot. When the tape robot is in motion, the current wall number is considered to be the number of the last wall accessed.
    Domain: wall numbers

5.4 Tape Robot.Desired Wall Number

The wall to which the tape robot is being directed. Under normal circumstances, the desired wall number will differ from the current wall number only when the tape robot is in motion. If, however, the robot is broken, it may stop before it reaches the new (desired) wall number.
    Domain: wall numbers

5.5 Tape Robot.Current Tier Number

The tier currently being accessed by the robot. When the robot is in motion, the current tier number is undefined.
Domain: tier numbers or undefined

5.6 Tape Robot.Desired Tier Number

The tier to which the tape robot is being directed. Unless the robot is broken, the desired tier number will differ from the current tier number only when the tape robot is in motion.
Domain: tier numbers

5.7 Tape Robot.Current Rank Number

The rank currently being accessed by the robot. When the robot is in motion, the current rank number is undefined.
Domain: rank numbers or undefined

5.8 Tape Robot.Desired Rank Number

The rank to which the tape robot is being directed. Unless the robot is broken, the desired rank number will differ from the current rank number only when the tape robot is in motion.
Domain: rank numbers

5.9 Tape Robot.Computer Name

Each tape robot is controlled by exactly one computer. This attribute provides the name of that computer, so formalizing the relationship Tape Robot IS CONTROLLED BY Computer.
Domain: Same as Computer.Computer Name

6. DRIVE

Drive (Drive Number, Density, Number of Tracks)

A Drive is a computer-controlled magnetic tape drive which is used to read and write industry-standard magnetic tapes for programs running on the computer to which it is interfaced.

Each tape drive in the computer center is assigned one of two roles: It can be acting as an operator-loaded drive, in which case it can be interfaced to any of the general purpose computers, or it can be acting as a robot-loaded drive. In this case, the drive must be interfaced to a computer that is equipped with a TSAR.

6.1 Drive.Drive Number

Each tape drive has been assigned a drive number which is used by the operations and maintenance staff to distinguish between the drives in service at the computer center.   The drive numbers are posted on the fronts of the drives.

Drive numbers are assigned from the integers by the maintenance group.

Domain: See above.

6.2 Drive.Number of Tracks

Each tape drive is equipped with magnetic heads which read and write bits in tracks longitudinally on the tape.   The number of tracks that can be read or written is determined by the construction of the magnetic heads and supporting electronics.

Domain: number of tracks (7 or 9)

6.3 Drive.Density

Drives may read and write data in a variety of densities, measured in bits per (longitudinal) inch of tape.   Standard densities available with the more modern drives are 800 bpi (bits per inch), 1600 bpi, and 6250 bpi.   The computer center also maintains a few older drives to allow access to tapes which were originally written at 200 or 556 bpi.

Some drives allow a choice of density.   Density selection, if available, is under computer control.

The Drive.Density attribute models the *set* of densities available on the drive.

Domain: [800 | 1600 | 6250 | 800 & 1600 & 6250 | 200 & 556]

7. OPERATOR-LOADED DRIVE

Operator-Loaded Drive (Drive Number, Computer Name)

Identifiers:

Drive Number

Description: An Operator-Loaded Drive is a magnetic tape drive that is not associated with a TSAR and, therefore, must have magnetic tapes mounted on it by an operator.

7.1 Operator-Loaded Drive.Drive Number

This attribute provides the drive number of the operator-loaded drive.   It formalizes the relationship Operator-Loaded Drive IS A (SUBTYPE OF) Drive.

Domain: Same as Drive.Drive Number

7.2 Operator-Loaded Drive.Computer Name

This attribute tells which computer the operator-loaded drive has been interfaced with. See the description of the relationship Drive IS CONTROLLED AND ACCESSED BY Computer.

Domain: Same as Computer.Computer Name

8. COMPUTER

> Computer (Computer Name, Manufacturer, Model Number, Serial
>   Number, Operating System)

Identifiers:

> Computer Name
>
> Manufacturer + Model Number + Serial Number

Description: The computer center operates a number of general-purpose computers for use by various departments of the company. Only general-purpose computers housed at the computer center and under the control of the operations staff are considered to be Computers in this model. Personal computers, network concentrators, and various special purpose machines do not qualify.

8.1 Computer.Computer Name

Every computer is assigned a name by the Operations Department. These names are in widespread use by operations, maintenance, and the computer users. The names are not posted on the machines, but appear on the Machine Schedule board in the user's lobby.

At one time the computers were named by a numbering system. Currently, however, they are named after Sesame Street characters: Big Bird, Oscar the Grouch, Cookie Monster, and the like.

Domain: See above

8.2 Computer.Manufacturer

This attribute provides the name of the manufacturer of the computer.

Domain: computer manufacturers

8.3 Computer.Model Number

The model number of the computer, as stated by the manufacturer.

Domain: manufacturer model numbers

8.4 Computer.Serial Number

The serial number given to the central processor by the manufacturer.
Domain: manufacturer's serial numbers

8.5 Computer.Operating System

The name of the operating system used on this computer when in production.
Domain: operating system names

9. TAPE REEL

Tape Reel (Tape Reel ID, Number of Tracks, Density)

Identifiers:

Tape Reel ID

Description: A Tape Reel is a magnetic tape which has been assigned a Tape Reel ID.

9.1 Tape Reel.Tape Reel ID

Each tape is assigned a unique identifier by the Operations staff before it is placed into service.   The identifier is of the form yy-mm-v-n, where yy are the last two digits of the year, mm is a one or two digit month number, v is a single letter code identifying the company division to which the tape will be allocated, and n is a sequence number assigned sequentially through the month.   The information encoded in the ID is purely for the convenience of the Operations staff, and is of no consequence to the usage of the tape.
Domain: See above

9.2 Tape Reel.Number of Tracks

The number of tracks written on the tape.   This attribute is established at the time the tape is first written ("initialized," in the terminology of the computer center). See description of Drive.Number of Tracks.
Domain: Same as Drive.Number of Tracks

9.3 Tape Reel.Density

The density at which the tape was written.   This attribute is established at the time the tape is initialized.
Domain: Same as Drive.Density

10. OPERATOR-ACCESSIBLE TAPE REEL

Operator-Accessible Tape Reel (Tape Reel ID)

Identifiers:

Tape Reel ID

Description: An operator-accessible tape reel is a reel of magnetic tape that is stored outside of the TSARs. Operator-accessible reels must be mounted on the operator accessible tape drives for use by programs.

10.1 Operator-Accessible Tape Reel.Tape Reel ID

This attribute provides the identifier of a tape reel that has been classified as an operator accessible tape reel.
Domain: Same as Tape Reel.Tape Reel ID

11. TSAR TAPE REEL

TSAR Tape Reel (Tape Reel ID, TSAR ID, Current Tape Location)

Identifiers:

Tape Reel ID

Description: A TSAR tape reel is a tape reel that has been placed in a TSAR.

11.1 TSAR Tape Reel.Tape Reel ID

This attribute provides the identifier of a tape reel that has been classified as a TSAR tape reel.
Domain: Same as Tape Reel.Tape Reel ID

11.2 TSAR Tape Reel.TSAR ID

At any time, a TSAR tape reel is to be found somewhere within the TSAR to which it has been assigned.
    This attribute, together with TSAR Tape Reel.Current Tape Location ID, formalizes the relationship TSAR Tape Reel IS CURRENTLY LOCATED IN TSAR Tape Location.
Domain: Same as TSAR Tape Location.TSAR ID

11.3 TSAR Tape Reel.Current Tape Location

This attribute tells which tape location within the TSAR currently holds the TSAR tape reel.

Domain: Same as TSAR Tape Location.Tape Location ID

12. TAPE MOUNT

Tape Mount (Mount ID, Date of Mount, Time of Mount,
Request ID)

Identifiers:

Mount ID

Description: A tape mount is the mounting of a tape reel on a tape drive for the purpose of access by a program.

Tape Mounts come in two types: Mounts done by an operator (formalized as Operator Tape Mounts) and Mounts done by a tape robot (formalized as TSAR Tape Mounts). This typing is reflected in the model by the subtype/supertype relationship between Tape Mount, Operator Tape Mount, and TSAR Tape Mount.

12.1 Tape Mount.Mount ID

An arbitrary identifier assigned to the Tape Mount for the purpose of formalizing the subtype/supertype relationship Operator Tape Mount/TSAR Tape Mount IS A Tape Mount.

Domain: See above

12.2 Tape Mount.Date of Mount

Every tape mount occurs on a date. This attribute reflects the date on which the mount took place.

Domain: dates

12.3 Tape Mount.Time of Mount

Every tape mount occurs at a specific time of day. This attribute records the time at which the mount took place.

Domain: times

12.4 Tape Mount.Request ID

Tape mounts are done at the request of a program that needs access to the tape. This attribute records the request that occasioned the mount. See also the description for the Tape Request object.
Domain: Same as Tape Request.Request ID

13. OPERATOR TAPE MOUNT

Operator Tape Mount (Tape Reel ID, Drive Number,

Mount ID)

Identifiers:

Mount ID

Description: An Operator Tape Mount is the mounting of an operator-accessible tape reel on an operator-loaded drive.

Operator Tape Mount is an associative object used to formalize the (Mc:Mc) relationship Operator-Accessible Tape Reel HAS BEEN MOUNTED ON Operator-Loaded Drive.

13.1 Operator Tape Mount.Tape Reel ID

This attribute tells which tape reel participated in the mount.
Domain: Same as Operator-Accessible Tape Reel.Tape Reel ID

13.2 Operator Tape Mount.Drive Number

This attribute tells which tape drive participated in the mount.
Domain: Same as Operator-Loaded Drive.Drive Number

13.3 Operator Tape Mount.Mount ID

This attribute formalizes the relationship Operator Tape Mount IS A (SUBTYPE OF) Tape Mount.
Domain: Same as Tape Mount.Mount ID

14. TSAR TAPE MOUNT

TSAR Tape Mount (Tape Reel ID, Drive Number, Mount ID)
Identifiers:

Mount ID

Description: A TSAR tape mount is the mounting of a TSAR tape reel on a robot-loaded drive.

TSAR Tape Mount is an associative object used to formalize the (Mc:Mc) relationship TSAR Tape Reel HAS BEEN MOUNTED ON Robot-Loaded Drive.

14.1 TSAR Tape Mount.Tape Reel ID

This attribute tells which tape reel participated in the TSAR tape mount.
Domain: Same as TSAR Tape Reel.Tape Reel ID

14.2 TSAR Tape Mount.Drive Number

This attribute tells which tape drive participated in the mount.
Domain: Same as Robot-Loaded Drive.Drive Number

14.3 TSAR Tape Mount.Mount ID

This attribute formalizes the relationship TSAR Tape Mount IS A (SUBTYPE OF) Tape Mount.
Domain: Same as Tape Mount.Mount ID

15. TAPE REQUEST

Tape Request (Request ID, Computer Name, Tape Reel ID,
Date, Time, Program Requesting)

Identifiers:

Request ID +   Computer Name

Computer Name +   Tape Reel + Date + Time

Description: Whenever a program requires a tape (other than a scratch tape), it issues a tape request. Each tape request specifies the particular tape required, the computer and program to which the tape is to be made available, and the time and date of the request.

Each tape request is eventually satisfied by a tape mount.

Tape Request is an associative object used to formalize the relationship Tape Reel WAS REQUESTED FOR USE BY PROGRAM RUNNING ON Computer (Mc:Mc).

15.1 Tape Request.Request ID

Each tape request within a particular computer is assigned a request ID—a number—by the operating system. This attribute records that request ID.
Domain: See above

15.2 Tape Request.Computer Name

Each tape request originates in a single computer. This attribute records the computer in which the request was generated.
Domain: Same as Computer.Computer Name

15.3 Tape Request.Tape Reel ID

This attribute tells which tape reel was being asked for in this tape request.
Domain: Same as Tape Reel.Tape Reel ID

15.4 Tape Request.Date

This attribute records the date of the tape request.
Domain: dates

15.5 Tape Request.Time

This attribute records the time of the tape request. It is assumed that time is recorded to such precision that a single tape reel cannot be requested twice at the same Tape Request.Time by programs running in the same computer.
Domain: times

15.6 Tape Request.Program Requesting

Every tape request is generated by a program. This attribute records the name of the program that generated the tape request.
Domain: program names

Part III: Relationships

1. TSAR HOUSES Tape Robot   (1:1)
Tape Robot IS HOUSED IN TSAR

Every TSAR housing comes equipped with a tape robot since this is necessary for the TSAR to accomplish the function for which it was designed. Every tape robot on site is installed in a TSAR.

The relationship is formalized by the referential attribute Tape Robot.TSAR ID.

2. TSAR CONTAINS Tape Storage Slot   (1:M)
Tape Storage Slot IS IN TSAR

Every tape storage slot, by definition, is a part of and inside exactly one TSAR. Each TSAR comes equipped with tape storage slots, since the tape storage slot is an essential aspect of the TSAR.

The relationship is formalized by the referential attribute Tape Storage Slot.TSAR ID.

3. Tape Robot HAS ACCESS TO TSAR Tape Location   (1:M)
TSAR Tape Location CAN BE ACCESSED BY Tape Robot

By construction of a TSAR, each tape robot has access to all the tape locations within a TSAR. Every tape location within a TSAR can be accessed by the tape robot that is contained in the TSAR.

The relationship is formalized by the attribute TSAR Tape Location.TSAR ID.

4. TSAR Tape Location IS A (SUPERTYPE OF) Tape Storage Slot
TSAR Tape Location IS A (SUPERTYPE OF) Robot-Loaded Drive

Tape Storage Slot IS A (SUBTYPE OF) TSAR Tape Location
Robot-Loaded Drive IS A (SUBTYPE OF) TSAR Tape Location

TSAR Tape Location is defined to be the union of all places within the TSAR in which the robot can place a tape. There are exactly two types of such places: the tape storage slots and the robot-loaded magnetic tape drives.

The relationship is captured by the combination of attributes TSAR ID and TSAR Tape Location ID, which occur in all three objects concerned.

5. TSAR IS ADJACENT TO Robot-Loaded Drive   (1:M)
Robot-Loaded Drive IS ADJACENT TO TSAR

In order for a TSAR to fulfill its function as a computer-controllable source of information from magnetic tapes, it must be equipped with at least one robot-loaded tape drive. The TSARs in use at the facility provide for several robot-loaded drives (4 or 6, depending on the model).

A tape drive is considered to be a robot-loaded drive only when it is installed adjacent to a TSAR, since it can be loaded by the tape robot only when placed adjacent to a TSAR.

The relationship is formalized by the referential attribute Robot-Loaded Drive.TSAR ID.

6. Computer CONTROLS Tape Robot   (1:Mc)
Tape Robot IS CONTROLLED BY Computer

Every tape robot is interfaced to one computer, under whose control the robot operates.   A given computer can control any number of tape robots.

The relationship is formalized by the referential attribute Tape Robot.Computer Name.

7. TSAR Tape Reel IS ASSIGNED TO Tape Storage Slot   (1c:1)
Tape Storage Slot IS ASSIGNED TO TSAR Tape Reel

Every tape reel that is placed in a TSAR for access is assigned a tape storage slot.   The tape reel is kept in the assigned tape storage slot whenever it is not mounted on a robot-loaded drive.

Each tape storage slot has, at most, a single tape reel assigned to it.

This relationship is formalized by the referential attribute Tape Storage Slot.Assigned Tape Reel ID.

8. TSAR Tape Location CURRENTLY CONTAINS TSAR Tape Reel (1:1c)
TSAR Tape Reel IS CURRENTLY LOCATED IN TSAR Tape Location

Each TSAR tape location can contain at most one TSAR tape reel at any given time.   Each TSAR tape reel is located in some TSAR tape location at any time.

This relationship is formalized by the referential attribute TSAR Tape Reel.Current Tape Location ID.

9. Tape Reel IS A (SUPERTYPE OF) Operator-Accessible Tape Reel
Tape Reel IS A (SUPERTYPE OF) TSAR Tape Reel

Operator-Accessible Tape Reel IS A (SUBTYPE OF) Tape Reel
TSAR Tape Reel IS A (SUBTYPE OF) Tape Reel

Each tape reel in the facility has been assigned to one of two categories: reels to be loaded by operators (in which case the reel is placed in the tape vault) and reels to be loaded by robots (in which case the reel is placed in a TSAR).

The relationship is formalized by the attribute Tape Reel ID, which occurs in all three objects concerned.

**10. Drive IS A (SUPERTYPE OF) Operator-Loaded Drive
  Drive IS A (SUPERTYPE OF) Robot-Loaded Drive**

**Operator-Loaded Drive IS A (SUBTYPE OF) Drive
Robot-Loaded Drive IS A (SUBTYPE OF) Drive**

The tape drives in the facility have been divided into two classes: those to be loaded by operators and those to be loaded by robots. Every drive is so classified.

The relationship is formalized by the attribute Drive Number, which occurs in all three objects concerned.

**11. Computer CONTROLS AND ACCESSES Drive   (1:Mc)
  Drive IS CONTROLLED AND ACCESSED BY Computer**

Every tape drive is interfaced to exactly one computer, while a given computer can be interfaced to zero or more tape drives.

The relationship is formalized by two paths, depending on the type of drive concerned. If the drive is an operator-loaded drive, the relationship is formalized by the referential attribute Operator-Loaded Drive.Computer Name. If the drive is a robot-loaded drive, the relationship is reflected in the model by a query chain: Robot-Loaded Drive.TSAR ID tells what TSAR the drive is adjacent to, Tape Robot.TSAR ID tells what tape robot loads the drive, and Tape Robot.Computer Name gives the name of the computer controlling the robot. This computer must be the one which is controlling and accessing the robot-loaded drive (or else we would be able to load a drive by a request from one computer, but not able to read the data from the tape).

**12. Operator Tape Mount IS THE MOUNTING OF Operator-Accessible
  Tape Reel ON Operator-Loaded Drive   M-(Mc:Mc)**

Operator Tape Mount is an associative object that is used to capture the (Mc:Mc) relationship Operator-Accessible Tape Reel HAS BEEN MOUNTED ON Operator-Loaded Drive. The (Mc:Mc) relationship is captured in attributes Operator Tape Mount.Tape Reel ID (which refers to an Operator-Accessible Tape Reel) and Operator Tape Mount.Drive Number (which refers to an Operator-Loaded Drive).

The underlying (Mc:Mc) relationship gives rise to an "incident" object: the mounting of the tape, which occurs at a specific time and date.

13. TSAR Tape Mount IS THE MOUNTING OF TSAR Tape Reel ON Robot-Loaded Drive   M-(Mc:Mc)

TSAR Tape Mount is an associative object that is used to capture the (Mc:Mc) relationship TSAR Tape Reel HAS BEEN MOUNTED ON Robot-Loaded Drive. The (Mc:Mc) relationship is captured in attributes TSAR Tape Mount.Tape Reel ID (which refers to a TSAR Tape Reel) and TSAR Tape Mount.Drive Number (which refers to a Robot-Loaded Drive).

The underlying (Mc:Mc) relationship also gives rise to an "incident" object: the mounting of the tape, which occurs at a specific time and date.

14. Tape Mount IS A (SUPERTYPE OF) Operator Tape Mount
Tape Mount IS A (SUPERTYPE OF) TSAR Tape Mount

Operator Mount IS A (SUBTYPE OF) Tape Mount
TSAR Tape Mount IS A (SUBTYPE OF) Tape Mount

Every mounting of a tape is done by either a robot or by an operator.

The relationship is captured in the model by the attribute Mount ID, which occurs in all three objects concerned.

15. Tape Request IS A REQUEST FOR USE OF Tape Reel BY PROGRAM RUNNING ON Computer   M-(Mc:Mc)

There is a (Mc:Mc) relationship between computers and tape reels, in that a tape reel can be requested any number of times by programs running on the computers. Similarly, a program can generate requests for any number of tape reels.

This (Mc:Mc) relationship is the basis for the associative object Tape Request, that formalizes the relationship by attributes Tape Request.Computer Name and Tape Request.Tape Reel ID.

16. Tape Mount SATISFIED Tape Request   (1c:1)
Tape Request WAS SATISFIED BY Tape Mount

A particular tape mount is generated in response to a single tape request. Every tape request will generate at most one tape mount. If the tape request is for a TSAR tape reel and if the computer for which the tape was requested does not have access to the TSAR containing the tape, the request will not be satisfied and no tape mount will occur.

The relationship is captured by means of the referential attribute Tape Mount.Request ID.

Appendix B

Data Organization
for a Real-Time
Process Control System

One way of storing data so that it can be accessed quickly by a number of separate processes is to put the data in a block of shared memory—memory that can be accessed directly by multiple programs. The following information model represents a scheme for organizing the data within that shared memory. The organization is based on tables, rows, and columns, so that as a result, the mapping between the application information model and the physical data organization is quite straightforward.

A data organization of the sort represented here is relatively easy to implement, since it depends only on a shared memory concept (common to real-time operating systems) and some method of binding the variables of the application code to the data organization. The binding method is necessarily language-dependent: Note that the language assumed here is FORTRAN.

PART I: Graphical Model

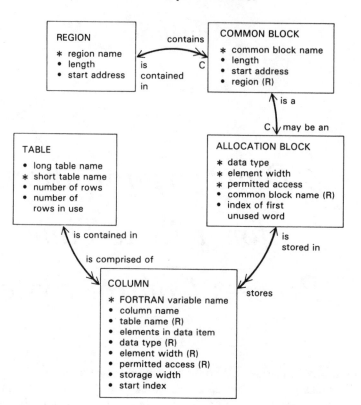

PART II: Objects and Attributes

1. REGION

Region (<u>region name</u>, length, start address)

Object Description: The region object models the global shared region (shared memory construct) of the operating system.

1.1 Region.Region Name

Description: Each global shared region which is generated is given a unique name by which it is known to the operating system. The region name attribute records this unique identifier of a global shared region.

Domain: Any legal global shared region name (operating system dependent, typically 1-6 alphanumeric characters).

1.2 Region.Length

Description: The length of the global shared region in words.
Domain: Operating system dependent, typically, a positive multiple of 256.

1.3 Region.Start Address

Description: The address in physical memory of the lowest-addressed word in the global shared region. [Mention here any operating system constraints, such as: This address lies on a page boundary.]
Domain: Machine and operating system dependent.

2. COMMON

Common (<u>common</u> block <u>name</u>, length, start address, region)

Object Description: The Common object models the "COMMON block within a global shared region" construct of the operating system/link-editor.

2.1 Common.Common Block Name

Description: A FORTRAN COMMON block is known to the link-editor by its name—the 1- to 6-character alphanumeric "label" of a labelled COMMON block.
Domain: FORTRAN COMMON block names

2.2 Common.Length

Description: The length of the COMMON block in words. The lengths are defined to be those acceptable to the link-editor: The lengths must be such that when taken together with the start addresses, no overlap occurs.
Domain: word count

2.3 Common.Start Address

Description: The address within the global shared region of the lowest-addressed word of the COMMON block.
Domain: physical word address

2.4 Common.Region

Description: The name of the global shared region that contains the COMMON block.
This attribute implements the relationship Region CONTAINS Common Block.
Domain: Same as that of Region.Region Name.

3. ALLOCATION BLOCK

Allocation Block (<u>data</u> <u>type</u>, <u>element</u> <u>width</u>, <u>permitted</u> <u>access</u>, common block name, index of first unused word)

Object Description: An allocation block is a unit of contiguous physical storage used to contain columns which are alike in certain ways: they are of the same FORTRAN data type, they require physical storage of the same granularity, and they require the same protection from destruction. The Allocation Block object models this implementation unit of the control system architecture.

3.1 Allocation Block.Data Type

Description: The FORTRAN data type of all data stored in this allocation block.
    Domain: real, integer, character, logical

3.2 Allocation Block.Element Width

Description: The size, in bytes, of the smallest element of data stored in this allocation block. This width is the measure of granularity for the block: how finely this block can be divided from the application's point of view. The element width does not take into account boundary alignment problems; that is, the element width of a character is 1, not 2.
    Domain: byte count

3.3 Allocation Block.Permitted Access

Description: The type of data access (reads and writes) allowed for the data in this allocation block. The permitted access attribute applies only to programs that have not been given special write access permissions.
    Domain: read only, read and write

3.4 Allocation Block.Common Block Name

Description: Each allocation block of the system architecture is implemented via a COMMON block. This architectural world relationship is modeled by the Common Block Name attribute, which records the name of the COMMON block.
    Domain: Same as Common.Common Block Name

3.5 Allocation Block.Index of First Unused Word

Description: Columns are placed in the allocation block starting at the lowest numbered address of the block. This attribute records where the next column

vector to be allocated may be placed.   Note that this is a FORTRAN index: It starts at 1 and advances by 1 for each separately addressable element of the allocation block.
  Domain: physical address

4. TABLE

Table (long table name, <u>short</u> <u>table</u> <u>name</u>, number of rows, number of rows in use)

  Object Description: All data in this system is perceived to be stored in tables consisting of rows and columns.   A relational view has been imposed on the data. The Table object models these tables.
  Note: The Table table is frequently called the "Table of tables"—an uncommon construction—to clarify descriptions.

4.1 Table.Long Table Name

Description: Each table has been assigned a name indicative of the world object it models.   Note that this is a name, rather than a description.   Legal long table names consist of as many as 30 alphanumeric characters.
  Domain: See above

4.2 Table.Short Table Name

Description: Each table in the system is assigned a unique two-character name for purposes of identification.   This short table name is an identifier for the Table object.
  Domain: See above

4.3 Table.Number of Rows

Description: The number of rows allocated for the table.   Every column that belongs to the table is allocated sufficient physical storage to contain exactly this number of elements.
  Domain: row count

4.4 Table.Number of Rows in Use

Description: Only a subset of the rows allocated for a table need be in use at any given time.   This attribute records the count of rows in use.
  Domain: row count

5. COLUMN

Column (<u>FORTRAN</u> <u>variable</u> <u>name</u>, column name, table name, elements in data item, data type, element width, permitted access, storage width, start index)

Object Description: The data in this control system is perceived to be stored in tables made up of rows and columns. Physical storage of the data is based on the columns of these tables. The Column object models the column vector, the fundamental storage construct for columns.

The Column table is referred to as the "Table of Columns," to parallel the "Table of tables" terminology.

5.1 Column.FORTRAN Variable Name

Description: Every column in the system has been assigned a unique 6-character name for purposes of direct access via FORTRAN. This name is a FORTRAN variable name (composed of letters and numbers only; the initial character is alphabetic); in addition, a number of conventions, described in the programming standards document for this project, rule the selection of the initial character of the name.

This attribute is an identifier for the Column object.

Domain: See above

5.2 Column.Column Name

Description: Associated with each column is a descriptive name, consisting of as many as 30 alphanumeric characters.

Domain: See above

5.3 Column.Table Name

Description: The name of the table to which this column belongs. This attribute implements the Table IS COMPOSED OF Columns relationship.

Domain: Same as Table.Short Table Name

5.4 Column.Elements in Data Item

Description: Associated with the intersection of a row and a column of a table is a certain amount of data, known as a data item. The data item may be simple (a single real number, or a character, for example) or more complex: a string of characters or a matrix of reals. An *element* is the smallest nondivisible unit of data contained in the data item.

This attribute gives the number of elements contained in each data item.

Domain: element count

5.5 Column.Data Type

Description: The FORTRAN data type of elements in this colunmn vector. This attribute, together with Column.Element Width and Column.Permitted Access, implements the relationship Column IS STORED IN Allocation Block.
  Domain: Same as Allocation Block.Data Type

5.6 Column.Element Width

Description: The size, in bytes, of a single element.
  Domain: Same as Allocation Block.Element Width.

5.7 Column.Permitted Access

Description: The type of data access (reads and writes) allowed for the column vector. The permitted access attribute applies only to programs to which special access rights have NOT been granted (that is, it applies to non-privileged programs only).
  Domain: Same as Allocation Block.Permitted Access

5.8 Column.Storage Width

Description: The number of bytes required to store a single data item (all of the data associated with the intersection of one row with this column). The storage width takes into account the FORTRAN boundary alignment rules, and hence is always an even number.
  Domain: byte count

5.9 Column.Start Index

Description: The index, within an allocation block, of the first element of the column vector. This is a FORTRAN index: It starts with one and advances by one for each separately addressable unit of data in the allocation block.
  Domain: FORTRAN index

PART III: Relationships

6. Region CONTAINS Common Block   (1:Mc)
Common Block IS CONTAINED IN Region

A global shared region can contain zero, one, or many COMMON blocks, while every COMMON block must be contained in one global shared region. This is a one-to-many conditional relationship (1:Mc). This relationship is reflected in the model by the attribute Common.Region, the domain of which is the same as that of Region.Region Name.

7. Common Block MAY BE AN Allocation Block   (1:1c)
   Allocation Block IS A Common Block

Each allocation block of the data architecture is implemented via a COMMON block. This relationship is reflected in the attribute Allocation Block.Common Block Name. Note that the relationship is conditional, reflecting the fact that there may be common blocks in the shared memory which are NOT allocation blocks. (These common blocks are used for system functions unrelated to the data architecture.)

8. Allocation Block STORES Column   (1:M)
   Column IS STORED IN Allocation Block

The STORES/IS STORED IN relationship is implemented by means of the attributes Column.Data Type, Column.Element Width, and Column.Permitted Access, which form a foreign key to the allocation block table.

9. Table IS COMPRISED OF Columns   (1:M)
   Column IS CONTAINED IN Table

The IS COMPRISED OF/IS CONTAINED IN relationship is implemented by the Column.Table Name attribute, which is a foreign key to the Table of tables.

Appendix   C

References

The following sources, most of which are widely available, are recommended for further reading.

PETER CHEN, *The Entity-Relationship Approach to Logical Data Base Design*, Q.E.D. Information Sciences, Wellesley, Massachusetts, 1977. There are also a number of other relevant papers in the literature by Dr. Chen.

E. F. CODD, A Relational Model of Data for Large Shared Data Banks, *Communications of the ACM,* 13, No. 6, June 1970.

C. J. DATE, *An Introduction to Database Systems*, Addison-Wesley, 1977. A standard text on databases. A more recent edition is available, but see Chapter 9 of the 1977 edition for a good discussion of normalization. Like other database works, this book does not focus on distinctions between the semantic (information) model and structural models.

TOM DeMARCO, *Structured Analysis and System Specification*, Yourdon Press, 1978. A popular and readable introduction to data flow diagrams.

MATT FLAVIN, *Fundamental Concepts of Information Modeling*, Yourdon Press, 1981. A formal, mathematically-styled treatment of information modeling. Fairly difficult. Treats semantic models only.

WILLIAM KENT, *Data and Reality*, North-Holland, 1978. Raises a number of questions illustrating the kinds of issues which arise in modeling the real world. The last part of the book is oriented around structural models.

JAMES MARTIN, *Computer Data-Base Organization*, Prentice-Hall, 1977. An easy-reading database book. Good for an overview of the subject.

JAMES MARTIN AND CARMA McCLURE, *Diagramming Techniques for Analysts and Programmers*, Prentice-Hall, 1985.

MEILIR PAGE-JONES, *The Practical Guide to Structured Systems Design*, Yourdon Press, 1980. One of the first on structured design, and still unsurpassed. Recommended.

D. C. TSICHRITZIS AND F. H. LOCHOVSKY, *Data Models*, Prentice-Hall, 1982. A survey book with a rich bibliography. Covers literature relating to both structural and semantic models.

JEFFREY D. ULLMAN, *Principles of Database Systems*, Computer Science Press, 1982. A standard database text, oriented towards structure and not semantics. Somewhat difficult.

R. VERYARD, *Pragmatic Data Analysis*, Blackwell Scientific Publications, 1984. Truly an information modeling book. Veryard claims that he has a hierarchical formalism in mind as a basis, but we were able to read this as if the underlying formalism was relational. Recommended.

EDWARD YOURDON AND LARRY L. CONSTANTINE, *Structured Design*, Yourdon Press, 1978.

Proceedings of the International Conference on Data Engineering, I.E.E.E. Computer Society Press, 1984. A wealth of ideas on both information and structural models.

Index

PROJECT TECHNOLOGY COURSES

OBJECT-ORIENTED SYSTEMS ANALYSIS: INFORMATION MODELING

Expands upon the ideas in the book. A case study based on a life-sized application enables students to become proficient with information modeling. Available in both real-time and business application versions.

OBJECT-ORIENTED SYSTEMS ANALYSIS: STATE AND PROCESS MODELING

Carries the methodology forward into a study of system dynamics. Techniques used include state models and data flow diagrams.

For more information about these and related courses, send inquiries to:

Project Technology, Inc.
2560 Ninth Street, Suite 214
Berkeley, CA 94710

Name _____

Company _____

Address _____

City _____ State _____ Zip _____

Phone _____

TEAR OUT THIS PAGE TO ORDER THESE OTHER HIGH-QUALITY YOURDON PRESS COMPUTING SERIES TITLES

Quantity	Title/Author	ISBN	Price	Total $
_____	Building Controls Into Structured Systems; Brill	013–086059–X	$32.00	_____
_____	C Notes: Guide to C Programming; Zahn	013–109778–4	$16.95	_____
_____	Classics in Software Engineering; Yourdon	013–135179–6	$37.33	_____
_____	Controlling Software Projects; DeMarco	013–171711–1	$36.33	_____
_____	Creating Effective Sofware; King	013–189242–8	$33.00	_____
_____	Crunch Mode; Boddie	013–194960–8	$27.00	_____
_____	Current Practices in Software Development; King	013–195678–7	$33.33	_____
_____	Data Factory; Roeske	013–196759–2	$22.00	_____
_____	Developing Structured Systems; Dickinson	013–205147–8	$32.00	_____
_____	Design of On-Line Computer Systems; Yourdon	013–201301–0	$47.00	_____
_____	Essential Systems Analysis; McMenamin/Palmer	013–287905–0	$32.00	_____
_____	Expert System Technology; Keller	013–295577–6	$26.95	_____
_____	Concepts of Information Modeling; Flavin	013–335589–6	$26.67	_____
_____	Game Plan for System Development; Frantzen/McEvoy	013–346156–4	$30.00	_____
_____	Intuition to Implementation; MacDonald	013–502196–0	$22.00	_____
_____	Managing Structured Techniques; Yourdon	013–551037–6	$32.00	_____
_____	Managing the System Life Cycle 2/e; Yourdon	013–551045–7	$33.00	_____
_____	People & Project Management; Thomsett	013–655747–3	$21.33	_____
_____	Politics of Projects; Block	013–685553–9	$21.33	_____
_____	Practice of Structured Analysis; Keller	013–693987–2	$26.67	_____
_____	Program It Right; Benton/Weekes	013–729005–5	$21.33	_____
_____	Software Design: Methods & Techniques; Peters	013–821828–5	$32.00	_____
_____	Structured Analysis; Weinberg	013–854414–X	$39.33	_____
_____	Structured Analysis & System Specifications; DeMarco	013–854380–1	$42.67	_____
_____	Structured Approach to Building Programs: BASIC; Wells	013–854076–4	$21.33	_____
_____	Structured Approach to Building Programs: COBOL; Wells	013–854084–5	$21.33	_____
_____	Structured Approach to Building Programs: Pascal; Wells	013–851536–0	$21.33	_____
_____	Structured Design; Yourdon/Constantine	013–854471–9	$48.00	_____
_____	Structured Development Real-Time Systems, Combined; Ward/Mellor	013–854654–1	$70.33	_____
_____	Structured Development Real-Time Systems, Vol. I; Ward/Mellor	013–854787–4	$32.00	_____
_____	Structured Development Real-Time Systems, Vol. II; Ward/Mellor	013–854795–5	$32.00	_____
_____	Structured Development Real-Time Systems, Vol. III; Ward/Mellor	013–854803–X	$32.00	_____
_____	Structured Systems Development; Orr	013–855149–9	$32.00	_____
_____	Structured Walkthroughs 3/e; Yourdon	013–855248–7	$23.33	_____
_____	System Development Without Pain; Ward	013–881392–2	$32.00	_____
_____	Teams in Information System Development; Semprivivo	013–896721–0	$26.67	_____
_____	Techniques of EDP Project Management; Brill	013–900358–4	$32.00	_____
_____	Techniques of Program Structure & Design; Yourdon	013–901702–X	$42.67	_____
_____	Up and Running; Hanson	013–937558–9	$28.67	_____
_____	Using the Structured Techniques; Weaver	013–940263–2	$25.00	_____
_____	Writing of the Revolution; Yourdon	013–970708–5	$37.33	_____
_____	Practical Guide to Structured Systems 2/e; Page-Jones	013–690769–5	$35.00	_____

Total $ _____

- discount (if appropriate) _____

New Total $ _____

OVER PLEASE ➡

AND TAKE ADVANTAGE OF THESE SPECIAL OFFERS!

a.) When ordering 3 or 4 copies (of the same or different titles), take 10% off the total list price (excluding sales tax, where applicable).

b.) When ordering 5 to 20 copies (of the same or different titles), take 15% off the total list price (excluding sales tax, where applicable).

c.) To receive a greater discount when ordering 20 or more copies, call or write:

Special Sales Department
College Marketing
Prentice Hall
Englewood Cliffs, NJ 07632
201–592–2498

SAVE!

If payment accompanies order, plus your state's sales tax where applicable, Prentice Hall pays postage and handling charges. Same return privilege refund guaranteed. Please do not mail in cash.

☐ **PAYMENT ENCLOSED**—shipping and handling to be paid by publisher (please include your state's tax where applicable).

☐ **SEND BOOKS ON 15–DAY TRIAL BASIS** & bill me (with small charge for shipping and handling).

Name _____

Address _____

City _____ State _____ Zip _____

I prefer to charge my   ☐ Visa   ☐ MasterCard

Card Number _____ Expiration Date _____

Signature _____

All prices listed are subject to change without notice.

Mail your order to: Prentice Hall, Book Distribution Center, Route 59 at
Brook Hill Drive, West Nyack, NY 10995

Dept. 1   D–OFYP–FW(1)